And Then We Were One - Real Solutions For Real Marriages

Published by Jentezen Franklin Media Ministries

PO BOX 315

Gainesville, GA 30503

jentezenfranklin.org

Cover design by Matthew Clark

Cover photo by Abbi Cooley, Images by Abbi.

Printed and bound in the United States of America

CrimsonInk **www.crimsonink.com**

AND THEN WE WERE ONE

REAL SOLUTIONS FOR REAL MARRIAGES

By Jentezen Franklin

TABLE OF CONTENTS

INTRODUCTION

I was talking to my wife Cherise recently and told her that I think one of the most difficult topics for me to speak on is marriage. I don't know why that is. We've been married a long time, but it's just so difficult. Typically, a person likes to speak about something they are more of an expert in, but I don't know any man who feels like he is an expert on marriage. No marriage is perfect, and there are things a person wishes that he could do over or words he could take back, so I take this subject very seriously. Perhaps it's the weight of the topic, knowing that so many marriages have failed, and there are many other couples who are still together but struggling greatly. This weighs on a pastor. The health of the families under the care of any pastor is a heavy responsibility.

Many books about marriage offer good, healthy advice. They teach processes, adages, counsel and a whole list of concepts that can lead to change ... eventually. But I am offering something different in the pages that follow. I believe God can do the miraculous in a moment! In a single second, with one decision—in a confession, repentance, or renewed commitment—God can change the course of your future. No advice or seven-step plan can compare to an encounter with the living God. That's what you'll find here. In each chapter ahead, a familiar chord will sound, and you will begin to see yourself, your spouse and your marriage through the eyes of our sovereign God. It is my hope that you will recognize some part of your life in a paragraph, a story or an illustration, and God will begin to bring clarity to the purpose in your relationship. Marriage is holy, ordained by God, and sacred in His eyes. Whether you are eager to perfect your good relationship, are striving to rekindle a lost connection, or are trying to hold on to what's left, God has a plan for your marriage. I believe through this book God can speak to YOU! At the end of each chapter, I encourage you to take a moment and hear God, reflect on what you've read, and invite the Holy Spirit to speak to your heart. Those moments, those encounters, can change everything.

I don't ignore the facts and statistics associated with marriage in the 21st century. Marriage itself is hanging in the balance, but I want to give you hope for your future. I want to reiterate that there is a plan and a purpose for marriage and, more specifically, for your marriage. Whatever condition your marriage is in, there are ways to move closer together, but it begins with God at the center. Here we will look at the many factors combatting marriage today, and we'll face those marriage-killers head on with each new chapter.

The amazing thing about our God is that anything and everything can change in a moment and in real and lasting ways. He says if we will just seek Him first, then put Him above everyone else, we won't need to worry. Move God to the center and then allow Him to work out your differences. Make God the focus and then trust Him to add everything else you need to the situation. When we consider the many dynamics that relationships contend with over time, it's no wonder so many fail. Two people, with the decisions and choices they make day in and day out, and the level of importance they place on their commitment to one another, cannot be trusted to go it alone. They need God. They need to have an experience with God that will shift the way they see things. If marriage is to be a success, it takes three, not two.

There is an enemy that has a very determined agenda, and destroying your marriage is high on his list of things to do. The good news is that for every marriage-killer and mountain he builds to discourage you, there is a Savior that stands ready to protect you. The Lord can remove every mountain and deflect every arrow of the enemy. I believe God is still performing miracles. I have this confidence because I have experienced it in my own marriage. I've seen it over and over again in marriages at every level, from happy and rejoicing, to bitter and broken. Our God is in the restoration business. He is rich in mercy, grace, and hope.

Marriage is God's idea. Healthy marriages are still the way He builds His church and exerts His influence over a lost and dying world. There is a purpose for your marriage, and He has a vested interest in seeing it succeed. The attack on family and marriage is evident. Too many believers are losing the battle, not because it can't be won, but because they can't see the path to victory. I want to help you succeed and make the marriage you're in the very best one God has ordained for you!

In the chapters of this book, we'll take a very honest look at the many issues that arise in marriages and examine practical ways to overcome these obstacles. You won't read a lot about perfect marriages with perfect plans and perfect outcomes. We'll examine real problems, from real people, in real marriages (including my own), and discover what makes them tried and true. Your marriage will test you, stretch you, and reveal things about you in ways no other relationship will. When the makeup comes off and the bills come calling, the best and worst parts of us are challenged! But I believe that with each trial, our faith has an opportunity to grow.

Scripture says that a cord of two is easily broken, but a threefold cord is unbreakable. Are you ready to see what this looks like in real life, every day marriage? I promise, if you are willing to invest and go all in, there is a way and there is a path that leads to joy in the journey.

Come with me through the pages to follow and learn what the great ones have learned through the ages: sometimes the greater the battle, the greater the victory. Victory is yours for the asking. One marriage, tried and true, is possible.

Section

01

One Marriage

CHAPTER 1

Marriage: As God Intended

> "
> Let marriage be held in honor among all, and let the marriage bed be kept pure, for God will judge the adulterer and all the sexually immoral (Hebrews 13:4).
> "

Marriage has followed many traditions throughout history. For example, did you know that, worldwide, more people get married in the month of June than any other month? That's not a new thing. The tradition of June brides dates back to the Roman Empire when they celebrated their god Juno and his wife Jupiter, the goddess of marriage and childbirth. In Victorian times, the tradition continued because June flowers were readily available for wedding décor, and the scent of the flowers masked body odor (a common problem of that time!).

Sadly, just as June weddings were rooted in the pagan culture of the Roman Empire, marriage today is being defined by worldly trends and humanist sociology. We find this God-ordained institution under attack from every side. All this was further complicated when one hotly contested legal verdict resulted in a deeply divided Supreme Court decision that legalized same-sex marriage in the United States. A new definition of marriage has emerged in our culture that looks something like this:

Marriage, also called matrimony or wedlock, is a socially or ritually recognized union or legal contract between spouses that establishes rights and obligations between them, between them and their children, and between them and their in-laws, as well as society in general. The definition of marriage varies according to different cultures, but it is principally an institution in which interpersonal relationships are acknowledged. When defined broadly, marriage is considered a cultural universal.

Marriage is beautiful. It is sacred and holy. It was never meant to be confusing, never meant to be ambiguous, and never meant to be redefined by man. Simply put, a marriage is the God-ordained union between a man and a woman where both pledge their love, their fidelity, and their lives to each other as long as they both shall live.

I realize that we live in a culture where many people choose to live together with no consideration of what the Bible says and think nothing of sleeping with someone (or multiple partners) before they are married. I know the majority of marriages in America end in divorce. That's why it is so critical for us to hear again and again God's plan and to be renewed in the truth of God's word as it relates to marriage.

There are many first-generation Christians who simply do not know the teachings of the Bible as it relates to marriage, fornication, and God's plan for sex. You may be one of them. Couple that with today's culture which embraces "anything goes," and it's understandable how easily carnality creeps into the most intimate and sacred of relationships. We must be intentional about protecting the vows of marriage.

Once when I was preaching at our Orange County, California campus, I challenged the congregation: "If you are living together, you just need to get married, and soon!" One couple came forward immediately, crying. They said, "We've been living together for over 10 years, and we've never been married. We have a little 6 year-old boy, and we don't want to mess this up. We want to get married. We want to get married tomorrow!" The boyfriend knew that he was about to be dealt with by God, if something didn't change. They were going through a very difficult time financially so my daughter Caressa, who is the co-pastor in OC, purchased some flowers and candles and turned this little room at the church into a beautiful wedding chapel. The next day, my son-in-law Ben performed a lovely wedding ceremony for this precious family.

"What greater thing is there for two human souls, than to feel that they are joined for life—to strengthen each other in all labor, to rest on each other in all sorrow, to minister to each other in all pain, to be one with each other in silent unspeakable memories at the moment of the last parting?" – George Eliot Secularism and Popular Opinion

We live in a fallen world, but we can work tirelessly to re-establish God's plan for love, marriage, and intimacy in a world where women and children have become a commodity and the marriage bed is exchangeable.

One very popular modern day secular life coach puts it like this:

I tell everyone I know that we need to re-define marriage…together as a society, individually as couples and every day. Question everything. Traditional "roles" are a lie. We made them up. And just like we made them up once, we can make them up again. So, question everything.

Another article, a Yahoo web-survey about sex and marriage and waiting until marriage to have sex, revealed a very casual approach among millennial respondents:

James:

I don't know. I mean those (religious) people are stupid, in my opinion. Even my parents say that is stupid. My dad says to test the waters first lol. I don't think it matters, but to me yeah my virginity mattered a whole lot. That's why I lost it to the person who I thought was the right one, and I was ready.

Others said the following:

Sandra:

I think you shouldn't have sex until you meet someone who you are really intimate with, like to the point where you're engaged almost. This way, if you do get pregnant, you know you have someone who you trust and can hold onto right next to you.

Nathan:

Honestly it doesn't matter if you're married or not. Religious fanatics and devout prudes will tout the importance of celibacy before marriage but I think it's more harmful than beneficial. It creates TONS of stress at wedding time, plus sexual intimacy has its own level of compatibility. People usually test drive cars before they buy them. The same should be done with a potential spouse.

Randall:

I didn't wait. I don't think it is only for marriage. I mean really I think marriage and sex ruin a lot of things. I'm all for sex before marriage, just don't be a slut about it.

A Healthy Historical Perspective

Before we get too sappy about the good old days or depressed about how bad things have become, remember that Christianity was birthed under the rule of one of the most immoral empires in the history of the world, the Roman Empire. Temple prostitution was common, as was homosexuality, pedophilia, and even bestiality. Jesus had to address divorce which had become so common in the early church because it had become socially acceptable in the culture. Once again, we find ourselves standing in the gap with the voice of truth compelling believers, young and old, to be separate from that world, to be salt and light, and to walk in a way that is counter to the culture.

On all of our Free Chapel campuses, our television ministry, and our conferences, God's plan for marriage and the family is a hill that we have taken a stand on and ground we refuse to surrender. Praise God, we are winning! In the last five years we have had thousands attend our yearly One Marriage Conference where marriages were restored, re-ignited, and reinforced; family trajectories were altered forever.

While the world is speaking out about all these crazy notions about marriage in the 21st century, I still believe God's word is every bit as real and valid today as it was when it was written some 2000 years ago. If you will allow God's word to penetrate your soul and become a central part of your marriage, what the world has to say will fade into the tragic statistics they are destined to perpetuate while your marriage thrives in all seasons of life. Let these verses be your guide and your public testimony:

> "So God created man in his own image, in the image of God he created him; male and female created them. And God blessed them. And God said to them, "Be fruitful and multiply and fill the earth and subdue it and have dominion over the fish of the sea and over the birds of the heavens and over every living thing that moves on the earth" (Genesis 1:27-28).

> Therefore what God has joined together, let no one separate (Mark 10:9).

> Enjoy life with the woman whom you love all the days of your fleeting life which He has given to you under the sun; for this is your reward in life and in your toil in which you have labored under the sun (Ecclesiastes 9:9).

> Above all, love each other deeply, because love covers a multitude of sins (1 Peter 4:8).

> *Be completely humble and gentle; Be patient, bearing with one another in love. Make every effort to keep the unity of the spirit through the bond of peace (Ephesians 4:2-3).*

> *And be kind to one another, tenderhearted, forgiving one another, even as God in Christ forgave you (Ephesians 4:32).*

> *Let marriage be held in honor among all, and let the marriage bed be kept pure, for God will judge the adulterer and all the sexually immoral (Hebrews 13:4).*

> *"For I know the plans I have for you," declares The Lord, "plans to prosper you and not to harm you, plans to give you hope and a future" (Jeremiah 29:11).*

We Are Winning This Battle

This stuff works! It really does. Every single week we have couples that come limping into our services, or just happen to turn on the television and find our Kingdom Connection program when they are at the end of a very, very short rope. There has been hurt, betrayal, and many times one or both have already decided that it is over and divorce is their only solution. They've tried what the world told them about marriage in this day and age, and it did not work. Then, they find that every step of obedience on their part is met by a God who is standing with open arms, a plan, and a hope for their future and the future of their family. We have witnessed couples breaking generational curses on marriages in their families, and then witnessed their children growing up in our programs on a very different trajectory than the one they were on previously. That is a hope that is extended to you with the turning of each new page.

Encounter

Our opinions, beliefs, and values take their shape from what we're taught, what we experience, and what we choose to accept as truth. Take a moment and ask yourself if you have held on to some mistruths about marriage and journal your responses.

Engage

What mistruths have you believed?

What truth, or scripture from this chapter, can you now stand on in your marriage?

What would you consider to be some of the most challenging experiences in your marriage and how did you navigate through them? What did you learn about each other?

In our first season of marriage we found out just how different we were. It got so bad one day that Cherise told her mother she wanted to come home. But thank God for a Godly mother-in-law! She told her, "Absolutely not." She told both of us that we needed to stay in this and work through those differences. She told us that we were being selfish. She was right, and over time we worked through those things.

Over the years I have learned the number one core value Cherise and I have to share is that divorce will never be an option. That changes everything, and especially the way you end an argument.

The Bible says:

For this cause shall a man leave his father and mother, and cleave unto his wife, and they two shall be one flesh. Ephesians 5:31

There has to be a leaving home . . . and a cleaving to each other.

CHAPTER 2

Biblical Roles—Ancient Parallels: Priests, Prophets, and Kings and Queens

> "
> A successful marriage requires falling in love many times, always with the same person.
> — Mignon McLaughlin
> "

Atmosphere, like temperature, can have a real effect on the home. Atmosphere is what a person feels or senses when they walk in a room. It's the sense of stability or the smell of fear. It's the lightness or heaviness you suddenly become aware of. According to scripture, as a husband, wife, dad or mom, you help create the atmosphere in your home based on the values you have chosen as your foundation. Unless the Lord builds the house, the builders labor in vain (Psalm 127:1). It doesn't matter what you do when you lead; if you don't understand the importance of atmosphere, then your plans will fail. You need to take that responsibility very seriously.

Professional athletes don't just show up and play. That would be foolish. No, there's preparation that sets the stage for success. From practices to pre-game rituals, attitude and mentality, laying the groundwork matters. So does inspiration, motivation, planning and an authentic love for the team.

The spiritual atmosphere of the home is the husband's responsibility. I begin every day of my life, with rare exception, in prayer. The first thing that comes off of my lips is this from Numbers 6:24-26: "May the Lord bless me and keep me, and make His face shine upon me, and may He make His countenance shine upon me, and give me peace." I go through that prayer every day, and then I start calling my children's names: Courteney, Caressa, Caroline, Connar, Drake, and my wife, Cherise. I plead the blood of Jesus, which is the protection of the Lord, over them. I am acting as their priest, going to God on their behalf.

Not only are husbands called to set the atmosphere and be the priest of their home, they are called to be prophets to their family. What did prophets do in the Bible? They represented God to the people. So not only do husbands and fathers represent their families to God through prayer and intercession, they also represent God to their family. Are you able to hear from God? That's what prophets did in the Bible. They heard from God and spoke the encouragement and exhortation God had for the people.

The Bible says in Genesis 6:8, "Noah found favor in the eyes of the Lord." God also warned Noah of things not seen, so Noah prepared an ark to save his family. His house was saved because he heard from God and knew what to do! We need fathers and heads of households like Noah. We need to pray and hear from God so that we may speak truth and wisdom to our families. We must have a sensitivity for our spouses, our children and those in our home to hear from the Lord on their behalf. Of course they can hear from God on their own, but even then, you are there to encourage them to *listen*. Your family could be saved based on what you have heard from God. Pay attention!

Being the head of the home is less about authority and more about responsibility. Men are called to be kings in their homes. The best kings are not self-serving and power hungry. The best kings are like our King Jesus—a servant who has the best interest of those he serves at the heart of every decision. As king, the husband rules on *behalf of God*. As king, he determines what happens in the home: what goes out, what comes in, who's invited, what's acceptable, what's not acceptable; he sets the boundaries that protect the home. A king establishes order and keeps it. A king protects his queen and leaves a legacy for his children.

As a father of five children (and not just one, but four daughters), I have to say that being king also means you have a say in who your children are friends with. You have a say about where they go, who they're with, and when they will be home. It is your responsibility to ask that young man standing at your door (and he better come to your door), "Where are you going? When will you be back? Do you understand what will happen if you're not back when you say you'll be back or if you go anywhere other than where you say you're going?" That's what dads do. That's what I did on more than one occasion, and that's what's missing in many homes today.

Fully Present Priests, Prophets, and Kings

My parents never asked me "Do you want to go to church tonight?" They TOLD me we were going to church! You may think that's a little old fashioned. BUT IT WORKED!! The Bible describes three functions of a father. The Bible said that the father is the PRIEST of the home, the PROPHET of the home, and the KING of the home. What does that mean?

As a PRIEST, one must ask, what does a priest do? In the Old Testament, the priest would represent the family before God. One of the functions of the father is to go before God on behalf of his family and represent his family before God. This is my responsibility as a father. In the Old Testament, when that death angel was passing by, God did not tell the mother, nor did He tell the children. He said, "Have all the fathers slay the lamb," and it was the fathers who were commanded by God to put blood on the doorposts. If the father ignored that command, the death angel would enter the home and kill the family. We, as fathers and husbands, are the priests of our homes, and it is OUR responsibility to lead and protect and provide. There is a death angel going through America, and we had better wake up and turn our families toward God before it is too late.

It is the PRIEST'S responsibility to represent his family before the Lord. If you are a single mom, or if the kids' dad isn't a believer, then you have to be both the mom and the dad and represent your family before the Lord. Every day of my life, with very few exceptions, I go and I pray somewhere and the first thing that comes out of my lips is, " Father, I ask you today to bless and to keep us," and I start calling my children's names out, "Courteney, Caressa, Caroline, Connar, Drake, and my wife Cherise. I plead the blood of Jesus over them." You know what I'm doing? I'm putting the blood on the doorposts, and I am the priest representing my family to God.

Discerning Prophets

The second thing that we, as husbands and fathers, are called to do is to be PROPHETS in our homes. What does a prophet do? **He represents God to the people.** So not only am I to represent my family to God in prayer and intercession as the priest, but I am also to represent God to my family. I need to be able to be present with God and hear from Him for every situation we encounter. Then it's my job to speak to my family about what I heard God say. That's what you need to be able to do, too. This is important. This is what the Word teaches!! Like Noah, DAD, your wife and your family will be saved based on what you have heard from God. Jesus, help us! We need men who know how to pray and HEAR from GOD and then speak to their families, men who have a sensitivity to their families to speak even the oracles of God.

Wives should not respect their pastor MORE than they do their husband, and children should not see more God in the man in the pulpit than they see in their own daddy. I'm going to say it again…if your family is only taught in a religious setting about their faith, then they will grow up separating religion from real life because they never heard it or saw it in the home. So MEN, you must start practicing it in the home! Oh Lord, give us godly homes with godly men as priests and prophets, ready to lay down their lives and their own selfish desires for the sake of their most precious possessions…their families.

Wise Kings

The last thing that we are called to do, as husbands and fathers, is to be KINGS in our homes. What does that mean? **"As King, the father rules the family on behalf of God."** That doesn't mean he's some kind of army sergeant. It simply means this: he decides and has authority about what's going to happen in that family.

Godly Queens

Proverbs 31 paints the portrait of a godly wife and mother. It says, *"Who can find a virtuous woman? For her price is far above rubies."* A husband and wife were celebrating their fortieth anniversary, and the wife said to her husband, "Why don't we go somewhere we haven't eaten in a long time?" The husband got her by the arm and walked her right into the kitchen! According to Proverbs 31 a godly mother knows how to make something for dinner besides reservations. Your virtue is what makes you priceless, and it's your job to instill this in your daughters.

The Scripture also said in Proverbs 31 that the great woman's lamp *'goes not out.'* In other words, she is a diligent worker. We all need to take our hats off to the housewives to ensure that their candles don't go out. The Scripture said that she's diligent about her work, and that means whether that be in the home or outside the home. She's not some welfare queen sitting on the couch eating potato chips, waiting on her check. In her tongue *'is the law of kindness.'* In other words, she's not a hell-raising woman that can cuss you out better than a marine drill sergeant. Her words produce happiness in her family and lift their spirits.

A Virtuous Woman

Proverbs 31 paints a portrait of the perfect wife and mother. It says, *"Who can find a virtuous woman? For her price is far above rubies."* Moms, you listen to me. Your virtue makes you priceless, so don't lose it on an altar of lust. Many a marriage has been lost in a moment of weakness.

It goes on to say, *"In her tongue is the law of kindness."* Say that out loud right where you are: *"In her tongue is the law of kindness."* Godly men and women produce godly children. And a kind word will go further than a word said in haste or anger every time.

Call on the Name of the Lord

We need the help of God if we are going to keep our marriages together and raise up godly children!! It was Joshua who said, "As for me and my house, we will serve the Lord!" Say that out loud right where you are:

As for me and my house, WE WILL SERVE THE LORD!

Right now, in this moment, everything can change. I really believe that. This isn't some self-help six-week plan that I am pitching. This is real life, right now supernatural change that brings with it a whole new hereafter. Allow me to pray this over you, and take it deep into your soul.

I pray this prayer over you: *Father, in the name of Jesus, I pray for every marriage and for every reader of this book; for every marriage that's needing Your help right now. I pray, Lord, that You would move in a mighty way in each home. It's not enough to go to church; they've got to see it in everyday life. I pray that a burden would come upon every husband, every father, that he would become the priest, he would become the prophet, he would become the king, of his home. I pray that the anointing of Proverbs 31 would come upon every woman and that she would be the ideal woman who glorifies You in the home, in her career, in her life, and through her womanhood, she would lead those children to Christ and honor that marriage vow.*

I pray for Your strength and Your help in our homes, that we would not fail at the most important mission that you could ever give us in life because the children that you have given us are eternal beings that will live somewhere one million years from now. May we, Lord Jesus, raise up a crop of godly children and godly families that bring Glory to Your Name. AMEN!

Your home is a classroom, you are the teacher, and the question is this: Will your children pass the grade? You need to give your family to God today. These are troubled times, and you don't want to be unsure about your walk with God in this critical hour in which we're living. You can't successfully build a home and a marriage in the atmosphere that we live in, an atmosphere of adultery, sin and perversion, without the power of the living God flowing through you. You need a clear mission of victory for your marriage and your family. You must have a sure foundation, and that foundation is Jesus Christ!

Encounter

Creating the right foundation and atmosphere is essential to a healthy, fulfilling marriage, but it begins with having Jesus at the center. Take a moment to journal below about the parts of this chapter that spoke to you personally:

....

....

....

....

....

....

....

Engage

Ask God to show you if there is anything you have put above Him in your marriage. What are some things you will do differently?

....

....

What can you do, beginning now, to ensure Jesus remains at the center of your relationship?

....

....

....

Real Solutions

What are the most difficult parts of marriage and how have you learned to keep your love alive?

The most difficult thing is just how different two people can be. Opposites attract, and this is where the fire and passion live. But that sure makes for some real differences of opinion sometimes. Marriage takes a ceremony and a signature. Relationship takes work—give and take, compromise. True love is when you realize just how different you are and you grow beyond tolerating each other to actually appreciating the differences. You come to realize, you really are better together.

Another challenging discovery is when you realize just how selfish you really are. I didn't feel like selfishness was an issue when I was single. I have learned over the years that, like all great challenges in life, marriage doesn't make you who you are, it reveals who you are. It's what we do with what we learn about ourselves that makes us more tender or more hard of heart. Selfishness is at the core of every marital problem. I wish I could tell you twenty ways to avoid being selfish, but it's a heart matter and it is deeply engrained through our habits and our routines. This is where your relationship to the Lord comes in. When you draw near to the Lord, it produces a mirror that reveals what you really look like to others . . . and to God, because He always sees what is true.

Make time for your relationship with the Lord. Take time to pray and read your Bible. Plant yourself in God's house and soon the rough edges will be revealed as God does a transformational work in your life.

The goal is always to look less like you, and more like Jesus.

CHAPTER 3

God's Word on Marriage and Family

> 66
>
> Happy is the man who finds a true friend, and far happier is he who finds that true friend in his wife.
> —Franz Schubert
>
> 99

Since the Garden of Eden, Satan has fought against the marriage covenant. But at every challenge throughout history, God had an answer and the marriage union still exists today, all over the world. Satan must have recognized it as a powerful union and a threat to him early on, because ever since he had an in-road through Eve, he has been able to introduce sins such as polygamy, pornography, adultery, fornication, homosexuality, prostitution and seduction. What an incredible thing to consider: everything that is prevalent in the 21st century was in the book of Genesis.

Genesis is the book of beginnings, and Satan starts in the very beginning hitting marriages and families with divorce, greed, and lust (just to name a few) to destroy them. That is why we must have godly marriages led by fathers who will be the priests, the prophets, and the kings of their homes, men who will stand up and cover their families and marriages in the blood of Jesus. Those who take the time to build their homes on the Rock of Christ Jesus will be able to weather the storms of life successfully and will have godly offspring.

I want you to understand two things that will paralyze a marriage: **ignorance and apathy.** A man was preaching on these very topics one night, 'ignorance and apathy,' and he pointed his finger down at one of the men on the front row and he said, "Isn't that right?" and the man on the front row responded, "I don't know and I don't care." That's the plague of our day! Far too many don't know and don't care because they're uninformed about the enemy trying to destroy our homes and our families.

You've heard that "opposites attract," but the truth is, and you need to understand that, after marriage, opposites irritate. You've also heard "It takes TWO to make a good marriage," but even that's not true! It really takes THREE. You cannot have a good marriage if you leave GOD out of your marriage! You show me a home where the husband loves the wife as Christ loves the church; you show me a home where the wife submits to the husband as the spiritual head as he leads spiritually; you show me a home where the children are obedient to the parents, and I will show you a happy home!

We have weak churches because we have weak families, and we have weak families because we have weak marriages. And we have weak marriages because we have weak husbands and fathers. And we have weak husbands and fathers because we have not trained them. Isn't that the truth?

Marriage Killer #1: Lack of Communication

One woman said, "I married my husband for better or for worse. He couldn't have done better, and I couldn't have done worse." I say that jokingly, but the reality is that 64% of divorces are caused by a lack of communication. Couples divorce because they REFUSE to communicate. **Lack of communication** is killing marriages, and so many times pride and selfishness is at the root of the issue.

One man was in a phone booth for 35 minutes with the phone up to his ear; he hadn't said a word...he just had the phone up to his ear. Another fellow waiting outside was getting upset. Finally, he beat on the door and said, "Listen, fellow, I've been standing out here 35 minutes. You've had that phone up to your ear the whole time and haven't said a word! Hang up the phone. You're not even using it and I've got to use the phone!" The man on the phone politely responded, "Excuse me, sir, I'm talking to my wife!" That is how far too many conversations go in our marriages.

One woman went to a lawyer for a divorce, and the lawyer asked her, "Do you have grounds?" She said, "About a half acre." He said, "No, I mean, do you have a grudge?" She said, "No, but I've got a carport." He said, "You're not understanding what I'm saying. Does your husband beat you up?" She said, "No, I usually get up about an hour before he does every morning." Finally, he said, "Lady, what is your problem?" She said, "My husband and I just can't communicate! We just can't communicate!"

For every unsuccessful marriage there is a successful marriage, and truth transcends time and space. There is a path that leads to joy, unity and peace. The gospels contain some of the most precious messages from that famous Sermon on the Mount which contained what are referred to as the Beatitudes. Just as Jesus preached the beatitudes for life, I would like to present a list of beatitudes for marriage.

Beatitudes for Married Couples

> Blessed are the husband and wife who continue to be affectionate, considerate, and loving all the days of their life.

> Blessed are the husband and wife who are as polite and courteous to one another as they are to their friends. (I've seen some men more courteous to another woman than they were their own wife, and vice versa.)

> Blessed are the husband and wife who have a sense of humor, for this will be a handy shock absorber.

> Blessed are the husband and wife who love each other more than any other persons in the world and will joyfully fulfill their marriage vow of fidelity as husband and wife.

> Blessed are the husband and wife who thank God for His blessings and set aside time each day for Bible reading and prayer.

> Blessed are the husband and wife who never speak harshly to each other and make the home a place of mutual encouragement and love.

> Blessed are the husband and wife who can work out their problems without interference from their relatives!!

> Blessed are the husband and wife who dedicate their home to the advancement of Jesus Christ, His Kingdom, and His Church!!

> Blessed are the husband and wife, in this day and age, who can live in harmony and with these Beatitudes in mind.

Marriage Killer #2: Taking Each Other for Granted

We were never intended to get our marriage advice from Dr. Phil, Oprah, or any other secular source! It comes from the **Bible!** It comes from **prayer,** and it comes from godly people that God places in our lives to help us do what the Scriptures say and not what our carnal mind tells us is acceptable according to our emotions. What happens is that after we get married, we have a tendency to take one another for granted. Today, if you see a man opening a car door for his wife, you can figure one of two things: he either has a new car or a new wife. Before a man gets married, he lies in bed at night thinking of what his beloved said. After he gets married, he falls asleep before she's finished saying it.

Marriage Killer #3: Selfishness

I Timothy 3 says that if a man who is physically and mentally able to do so does not provide for his family, *"He denies the faith and is worse than an infidel"* (**I Timothy 5:8**). America is saturated with deadbeat dads who sire children with their latest lover and then leave, never to be seen again, while that child grows up absent one of the most critical relationships he or she will need: a loving, caring, nurturing, and providing dad. That is NOT sexual freedom; that is moral insanity, and the Bible says that this kind of person has no religion at all. If you have children, you are responsible for those children, or else you deny the faith and you are WORSE than a heathen. Hollywood projects single motherhood as glamorous, but real life single moms will tell you it is anything but exciting. It is the hardest thing they will ever do.

One half of all single mothers live below the poverty level. One half!! Understand that one of the Biblical names of God is Jehovah Shammah. The word "Shammah" means "THERE." The God Who is THERE! And there are too many fathers who are NOT "there" in their children's lives. And if God is our heavenly Father, and He is there, you should stay there and be actively involved in your children's lives.

Marriage Killer #4: Disengaged Fathers

You actually don't have to move out to be an absentee father. Some of you dads who are reading this were amening me when we were talking about those deadbeat dads who move out and never come back, but the fact is that there are a lot of selfish dads who live at the house but aren't really there. The average dad in America spends two minutes a day in meaningful conversation with his children. *Two minutes a day!* 79% of the people who are addicted to drugs, according to Bill Bennett's book, started taking them because of a void that was created from a fatherless home! Well, I had a drug problem when I was a child. I don't like to talk about it, but I had a serious drug problem. I was 'drug' to church every Sunday morning. I was 'drug' to church every Sunday night, and I was 'drug' to church every Wednesday night. I was 'drug' to prayer meeting. I was 'drug' to the woodshed when I got out of line, and Daddy beat my tail. I was 'drug' to a lot of places and it was those 'drugs' that got into MY veins. Those kind of 'drugs' are stronger than cocaine, heroin, marijuana, meth, or anything else, because my parents had sense enough to drag me to God's house!!

Blood Lines and Generational Curses

Godly men and women produce godly children. In New York state there was a man by the name of Max Dukes. He was raised by agnostics, and never taken to church in his life. No church. No God. He had never been taught to fear, serve, love God, read the Bible, or pray. Max Dukes had 1,026 members of his family tree that had never darkened the doorway of a church, and in fact, 300 of them went to prison for an average of 13 years, 190 became public prostitutes, and 680 out of the 1,026 became alcoholics. It cost the state of New York millions to take care of them.

BUT growing up at the exact same time, in exactly the same town, was a man by the name of Jonathan Edwards, a man who would become a powerful puritan preacher. Jonathan Edwards had 929 descendants in his family tree. Out of the 929 descendants from this man there came 430 preachers, 86 college professors, 13 presidents of major universities, 75 best selling authors, 7 members of the United States Congress, and one member became Vice President of the United States of America!!

We need the help of God if we are going to keep our marriages together and raise godly children!! It was Joshua who said, "...*as for me and my house, we will serve the LORD!*" What about your house? You may be married with children or married with no children, but either way you have a decision to make. As for you and your house... what? How will YOU TWO complete that sentence? Everything really does depend on that resolve and that "made up mind." That sentence is the most important question you will ever have to answer. As for me and my house...you fill in the rest. Choose wisely.

Allow me to pray this prayer over you. As you read it, allow it to settle deep into your soul.

In the name of Jesus, I pray for every marriage that's needing Your help right now. I pray, Lord, that You would move in a mighty way in the home of everyone reading this book. Help us to remember that only godly parents raise godly children. Only godly husbands and wives make for good marriages. It's not enough to go to church and do and say all the right things when we are in public; we've got to live it in everyday life. I pray that a burden would come upon every husband, every father, that they would become the priest, they would become the prophet, they would become the king of their home. I pray that the anointing of Proverbs 31 would come upon every woman, and that she would be the ideal woman that glorifies You in the home, in her career, in her life, and through her womanhood, she would lead those children to Christ and honor that marriage vow, because godly men and women make for godly homes and marriages.

Encounter

Which of the four marriage-killers do you feel pose the most threat to your marriage?

Engage

I challenge you to write down three things you can do to improve this area of your marriage.

Real Solutions

How do you keep love alive?

This may surprise you, but one answer is simply giving each other some space. Cherise and I have learned to give each other space, and it's the space that makes the together time that much more fresh and meaningful. We aren't apart that much, but when we are together we don't smother each other. We also make time to get away, just the two of us where we can have alone time and just focus.

We've also learned to keep the main thing the main thing. All the television I do, the books, the conferences, and leading a multi-campus church are important, and the Lord moves in powerful ways. But the main thing above all, is my wife and my family. I always take those calls. We spend time on both coasts because that is where our family is, so we make it a priority to be with family.

You have to make the main thing the main thing, and don't let life dictate your priorities.

Section

02

Man of God—Woman of God

INTRODUCTION

From the very beginning, God created man and woman to be very different. It was always His intention in creating a "helpmate." Though we are uniquely different from one another, we are better together. We can be more focused on being independent and having things our own way than the "together" part. And let's face it, good relationships require a desire to work together even if that takes more effort.

In that same vein, the unity in marriage cannot deny or try to diminish the thought that it was God's idea to create us uniquely different. When we spend all of our time trying to eliminate the distinctions between the two sexes we find that only the similar parts are allowed in the relationship, and it is inevitable that brokenness and hurt will take place because ultimately God's design for man will cry out from the depths of his soul...to be fully man, and from a woman to be uniquely woman. So rather than trying to get your spouse to be more like you, or vice versa, it is far wiser in a relationship to present the very best version of "you" while growing closer to the Lord in your daily walk, your behavior, and the choices you make.

Often times, we can spend all of our time trying to constantly grow closer to our spouse while neglecting the development and health of our relationship with the Lord. In actuality, it would be far wiser to place your focus on growing closer to the Lord, knowing if you are both drawing near to Him, you are in fact growing closer to each other. It's all geography...in the Spirit.

Opposites attract, and they always have. And there are three paths to choose from when it comes to relationships of any kind, and especially marriage. Option One: They must become more like ME. Option Two: We must let go of the things that make us so different and only live in that zone that includes the things that we have in common. Too often we take only the parts of our spouse that we like...and vice versa including friends, family, hobbies, interests, work schedules, and other things. And then there is Option Three: You celebrate and embrace what is different and give your challenges to the Lord, while focusing on your own relationship with the Lord and encouraging your spouse in their walk with Jesus. Constantly interceding, loving, caring, and being more like Christ.

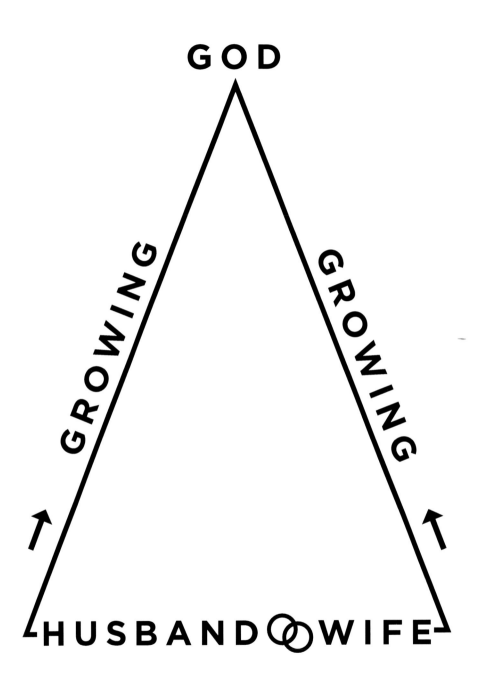

Scripture often refers to the church as the bride of Christ; a very powerful image of the closeness, love and devotion the Lord has for His people. In Ephesians chapter 5, the Word gives a very strong challenge to husbands:

Husbands, love your wives, just as Christ loved the church and gave Himself for her.

What a powerful word, and what a specific and unique role the Lord gives to a husband.

Then in Proverbs chapter 31 it says of the wife:

An excellent wife who can find? She is far more precious than jewels. The heart of her husband trusts in her, and he will have no lack of gain. She does him good, and not harm, all the days of her life.

The role of the wife in shaping the destiny of a marriage and a family is completely unique and powerfully influential.

The next five chapters were written with these two unique designs in mind. One was written focused on men and the other on women. Read both. The goal is for you to see yourself and your role in both sections...knowing that while you are both uniquely different, in God's plan you are better together.

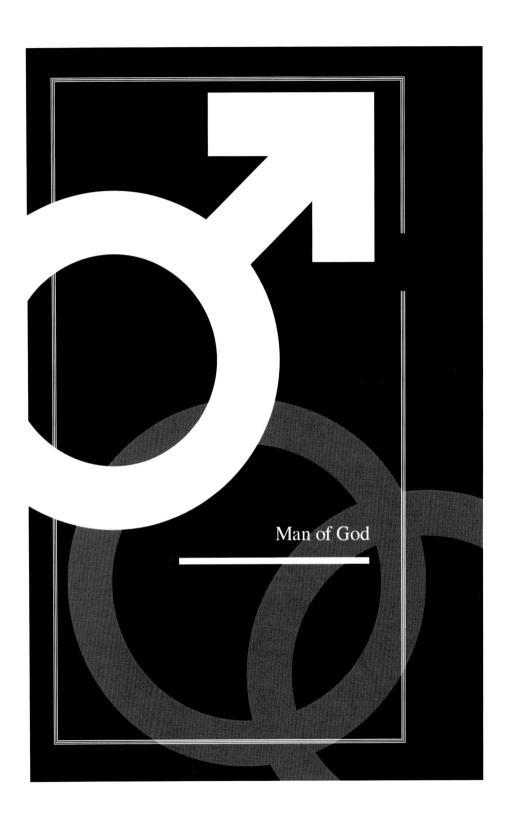

Man of God

CHAPTER 4

Be of Good Courage

"

Don't marry the person you think you can live with; marry only the individual you think you can't live without. —James Dobson

"

"Be of good courage, and play the man," comes from a great story in II Samuel 10:1-13:

In the course of time, the king of the Ammonites died, and his son Hanun succeeded him as king. David thought, "I will show kindness to Hanun son of Nahash, just as his father showed kindness to me." So David sent a delegation to express his sympathy to Hanun concerning his father.

When David's men came to the land of the Ammonites, the Ammonite commanders said to Hanun their lord, "Do you think David is honoring your father by sending envoys to you to express sympathy? Hasn't David sent them to you only to explore the city and spy it out and overthrow it?" So Hanun seized David's envoys, shaved off half of each man's beard, cut off their garments at the buttocks, and sent them away.

When David was told about this, he sent messengers to meet the men, for they were greatly humiliated. The king said, "Stay at Jericho till your beards have grown, and then come back."

When the Ammonites realized that they had become obnoxious to David, they hired twenty thousand Aramean foot soldiers from Beth Rehob and Zobah, as well as the king of Maakah with a thousand men, and also twelve thousand men from Tob.

On hearing this, David sent Joab out with the entire army of fighting men. The

Ammonites came out and drew up in battle formation at the entrance of their city gate, while the Arameans of Zobah and Rehob and the men of Tob and Maakah were by themselves in the open country.

Joab saw that there were battle lines in front of him and behind him; so he selected some of the best troops in Israel and deployed them against the Arameans. He put the rest of the men under the command of Abishai his brother and deployed them against the Ammonites. Joab said, "If the Arameans are too strong for me, then you are to come to my rescue; but if the Ammonites are too strong for you, then I will come to rescue you. Be strong, and let us fight bravely for our people and the cities of our God. The Lord will do what is good in his sight."

Then Joab and the troops with him advanced to fight the Arameans, and they fled before him.

It's Time To "Play The Man"

I believe the Lord is looking at the times in which we're living and He is saying that there has never been greater opposition to the family, to the marriages, to the homes, to our children, to our finances, or to our nation. What are we going to do? There's an onslaught that's come against anyone and everyone who stands for what the Bible teaches. If you haven't felt it, hang on, it'll come to your house sooner or later! What are we going to do? I believe all of Heaven is looking to us … to the church, and saying to the men, "It's time to 'Play the Man!'"

I am a pastor for sure, but I have to tell you right now that I'm living my life for Courteney, Caressa, Caroline, Connar and Drake, my five children. I'm also living my life for Cherise, my beautiful wife. I'm living my life for the people of the congregations in my churches, and the people that He's given us to minister to through the outreaches of this church and our television ministry.

I'm living my life for the town where I live. I don't know why He assigned me here, or why He assigned me to go all over the world. But as long as I am here, then I'm supposed to make a difference in people's lives in my city, in my nation, and in the world. I want to ask you this simple question: Who are you living YOUR life for?

Hugh Letterman was a 16th century English Bishop who preached so strongly against the sin of his time that the authorities put him in prison in the Tower of London and locked him up along with his colleague, Nicholas Wrigley, another evangelist. They stayed there for months, literally starving. They finally brought him and his associate out to be burned at the stake for their beliefs and insistence on standing against sin.

As they prepared a stake where they would burn him alive for preaching against the sins of the people, he said, "Somebody needs to pray for me. All the power that I have felt seems to have waxed away. But if somebody will pray for me, I know God will help me."

As they were tying the two men to the stake, he turned to Wrigley and said, "Master Wrigley, please today, we must **play the men**!" What a powerful moment as all of Heaven, and history, looked on.

Letterman went on to say, "Master Wrigley, we shall this day light such a candle in England that I trust it will never be put out." When they lit those human candles on fire, their flesh began to burn because they would not renounce what they believed in the Word of God and the name of Jesus Christ. Everyone there saw the courage and the passion of the few who would dare to "play the men" in their moment of decision and in their public testimony. That's where that statement has its origin in modern history, but we know that the real origin is from the passage in II Samuel Chapter 10.

They were singing a hymn of praise as they were being burned alive, as they were **"Playing the Man!"** That's amazing! Ever since that time to this, that statement **"Play the Man"** has simply meant this: Whatever happens in your life, whatever comes at you during the course of a day, refuse to grovel at the feet of your enemies. We Christians do not let the enemy see us sweat. We do not throw up our hands in despair and quit; we do not cave in. We stand and we "play the man." Today we stand on the Word of God and we **"Play the Man!"** We say **"Greater is He that is in me than he that is in the world!"** I personally know what it means to go through a very difficult time. Being a pastor does not protect me from the trials of life and the attacks of the enemy, but I have determined that when I'm going through something, I'm going to **"Play the Man!"**

Marriage in the 21st century is no easy matter. You may be reading this today and you are discouraged, and you feel the weight of the world on your shoulders. You feel you are without hope. You feel like you're so low you could crawl in a mouse hole and have room left over. The Lord told me to tell you to **"Be strong and courageous!"** You were just laid off and you don't know what you're going to do? Behind on your payments? Received a bad medical report? Trouble with one of your kids? Ever feel like you're about to have a nervous breakdown? Don't give up and don't give in. We all find ourselves in these situations at different times, but I'm here to shake you and say **"Be**

strong and of good courage, and Play the Man."

Stand up for that family, Dad. Stand up right in the middle of all that hell and say, "I'm not leaving! I'm not going anywhere! We're going through some junk, but we're going to get through it. Though we walk through this valley, we will get through it! I'm going to 'Play the Man' for my family! I'm going to 'Play the Man' for my community. I'm going to 'Play the Man' for myself, and I am going to 'Play the Man' for my God." I grow so weary of tired, weak, pitiful Christians! We all have junk. We all have problems. Be strong and courageous and Play the Man!

The Bible says that when David heard his friend Nahash, the king of the Ammonites, had passed away, he sent an encouraging word to Nahash's son Hanun, who would inherit the throne. He had one word: peace. You know, our King has the same message for a troubled, messed up world – **"peace."** Can't sleep at night because you're so worried? – "peace." Trouble in your family and your marriage? – **"peace."**

But the Bible says, "Hanun did not receive or accept that message and turned on the messengers of David and severely mistreated them." If ever we needed to pray for the messengers of OUR King Jesus in the 21st century, it's now! Notice that Hanun put his attack on the messengers! If ever you needed to pray for your pastors and your spiritual leaders, it is now, because the enemy hates the messengers.

The Bible says that Hanun didn't kill them because he didn't have that kind of power. He tried, but he just was not able. Instead, Scripture says, *"He captured the messengers that brought good news, and rejected their message. And then he shaved half the beard off."* You see, in the Old Testament, the beard identified a free man from a slave. In the Old Testament, only slaves were shaved under the Old Covenant. A slave was not allowed to wear a beard; if a man had a beard he was a free man. But Hunan didn't just cut off their beards; the Bible says that, *"He then cut their tunics"* which represented the covering that they were under. Hanun had their tunics cut off at the waist so that these men were not only humiliated by shaving off half of their beard, but he then exposed them to the whole world to be mocked and laughed at to bring them great shame.

This is what Satan wants to do to you, too. Satan was saying to these men, "I can't take all your freedom because **'He whom the Son sets free, is free indeed.'"** Now, you may have some issues in your life, but if you've given your life to Jesus Christ, Satan cannot take your freedom! Never forget these priceless words from Jesus in John Chapter 8, "Therefore, if the Son makes you free, you shall be free indeed" (v 36). However, Satan will always seek to limit your liberty.

What I love most about this story is that even though Hanun humiliated the servants of David, it did not change David's opinion one iota of who his messengers were. As a matter of fact, when the men returned to David with the bad news of disgrace to the messengers, David sent his men out immediately to intercept them. He didn't want them to come home and be shamed. He didn't want them to come back and be embarrassed. That is the heart of a true king. He said, "*I want you to go out and meet them and take them down to another city called Jericho.*" Jericho means, "*fragrant place.*" Even though they've been shamed and the enemy has tried to take their freedom by telling them 'they don't belong, they're outcasts, they'll never be free,' David made sure that these men WILL be able to hold their heads high again.

This story is reminiscent of the story of the prodigal son in the New Testament. When the father heard that his son was coming home from the pigpen, he said: "*Oh, give me a robe, give me some shoes. I can't let him come home and everybody see his shame. Let me run out.*" The father grabbed the coat and sandals, and ran. "*But when he was still a great way off, his father saw him and had compassion, and ran and fell on his neck and kissed him*" (Luke 15:20). The only time in the Bible that you find that "God ran" was when He ran out to find an old backslider!

Our heavenly King, Jesus Christ, believes in restoration. I believe in restoration. I believe in a restoring God full of forgiveness, grace, and mercy. I have talked a lot in this chapter about "Playing the Man" and most men have failed in one way or another. Maybe you are reading this feeling like a complete failure. **God has sent me to tell you that you are never too far from God's grace and mercy to find forgiveness.** He wants to restore you and renew your strength. You cannot 'play the man' in your own strength. Just like those two precious pastors burned at the stake after praying for each other, nothing is possible in our own strength; we must be strengthened in the Lord.

Take a moment right where you are and come before the Lord in prayer and humility and complete transparency. Tell Him where you have failed. Confess it and ask God to cover it with His blood. He will. Repent and turn away from those deeds and ask Him to renew your strength by renewing your faith. Then allow His presence to come over you, cleanse you, restore you, and renew your strength. You have a wife that is counting on you to "Play the Man." You have a family counting on you to "Play the Man." It's time to step up and stop playing games with God. Today is your day to change everything and start "Playing the Man."

Marriage today requires an extraordinary commitment, but that does not come without help from a God who is for you and who is with you and who will provide what you need, exactly when you need it if you will simply call out His name. He IS your very present help in times of trouble. He is your strong tower, and He is for you. Play the man...and trust the rest to Jesus.

Encounter

We have all made mistakes and choices that we wish we could take back. But we can only move forward. Before you can truly move forward, you must humble yourself and repent. Right now, ask God to show you your wrong actions, words, thoughts, or feelings that are affecting your marriage.

....

....

....

....

....

....

....

Engage

If the Holy Spirit prompts you to apologize, confess, or simply share these things with your spouse, you certainly should. Sometimes we hurt others unintentionally, and asking for forgiveness could be key in moving forward.

Take a moment to reflect on what God would have you to do.

....

....

....

....

....

....

Disagreements and potential arguments are a part of marriage life, but how do you handle serious arguments in your marriage?

We have a real marriage, and we lead real lives just like you. We have had some real knock-down-drag-out arguments . . . just like you have. It's called being a human with a mind of your own. But we determined in our hearts a long time ago, that those times of disagreement, hurt or anger would not define us. From the very beginning we have said that separation and divorce are simply never going to be an option in this marriage. Not even a possibility. Making that declaration is critical to how you come to view those tough conversations. We try not to take ourselves too serious.

We have learned a couple of very valuable lessons over the years: things always look different in the morning, and there is a little bit of fault in both sides of just about every argument. We as humans are selfish by nature and there will always be war with the flesh. I can honestly look back at some big arguments we have had and today they seem so meaningless that we can't believe we ever got so upset. The Bible says:

Be angry, yet do not sin; do not let the sun go down on your anger. Ephesians 4:26

CHAPTER 5

Wake Up the Mighty Men to the High Call of Marriage

66

Battle is the most magnificent competition in which a human being can indulge. It brings out all that is best; it removes all that is base. All men are afraid in battle. The coward is the one who lets his fear overcome his sense of duty. Duty is the essence of manhood. —George S. Patton

99

In over 27 years as a pastor and over 30 years in the ministry, I have learned that men respond to straight talk. Men like for people to deal with real issues and tell it like it is. Men don't need to be talked 'at' about stuff that they can't even relate to. With me, my ADD kicks in quickly if I can't relate to what a speaker is talking about. When I'm reading my sermon outline, I know that if it's boring me, then I don't have a shot with most of the men. For far too many men, this is what they see in church, and what causes many of them to opt out.

We need to equate faith with guts. Ladies, if you can find ways to show your man that being a part of a faith community does not mean they have to get in touch with their feminine side, you may have a shot at getting them to church. The church, in far too many cases, has feminized the church experience, and we have stopped relating to and speaking to real men. Men need preaching that challenges men and connects with men. We need to call men to commitment. Why? Because boys follow men!

Proclaim this among the nations:

"Prepare for war!

Wake up the mighty men,

Let all the men of war draw near,

Let them come up.

Beat your plowshares into swords

And your pruning hooks into spears;

Let the weak say, 'I am strong'"(Joel 3:9-10).

"Wake Up The Mighty Men." Ninety percent of the men who live in the United States say they believe in God. Five out of six men in the U.S. refer to themselves as "Christians." Yet only 35% of the men in the United States attend church. Only 35%! Only one out of five women will have their husband sitting beside them in church today. I look out over the congregations I preach to, in churches all over the world, and so many of the women in each service will not be sitting with their husbands. It's a startling statistic! Why?

I refuse to believe that Jesus Christ, one of the toughest men ever to walk this earth, is not relevant to the 21st century man. But I do believe that there's a total disconnect between many men and the 21st century church experience, especially in the American culture. Men outnumber women in the Hindu faith. Men outnumber women in the Buddhist faith. Men outnumber women vastly, greatly in the Islamic faith. Only in Christianity do women outnumber the men.

So what is going on? Why is there an absence of "manly men" in the church? Where are the risk takers, the rough and tumble strong men of God? There must be a place for men in our churches. There must be a place for "real guys" in the church. It is so critical that we find answers to these questions or we will continue to have churches filled with women without their husbands. Maybe that describes you or your husband.

I have often thought that most men in the Bible wouldn't fit in our churches today. Think about Moses. The Bible says that he was the leader of the nation of Israel. But can you imagine somebody interviewing him for that pastorship and asking, "What did you do before you became a pastor?" Moses would say, "I murdered a guy, and buried him in the sand."

I'm not advocating violence here; I'm just telling you God used real men in the Bible! Manly men! Men like Elijah who got mad and said, "You mess with me and I'll call down fire from Heaven and burn you up!" And then he DID it!

God used men like the mighty men of David. He had warriors that would spit and grass would die. They could kill a thousand men. One man killed a thousand Philistines with an ox goad. I thought about Peter who was packing a blade. Remember, when they came to arrest Jesus, Peter pulled out the blade and WHACK! With one stroke he cut a guy's ear off. Jesus asked Peter why he did that. He did it because Jesus was his leader and his friend. That's just the kind of men they were. Real men! Jesus wants you to be a real man. The church of the first century was a magnet to men. Jesus' ministry was a magnet to men, and they were drawn to it. They liked it. They couldn't wait to get around it and be a part of it.

The Disciples

When Jesus officially started His ministry, one of the first things He did was to find twelve men. Jesus took those twelve men and turned the world upside down. Jesus, a carpenter by trade, chose fishermen, a business leader, a tax collector, and a doctor. He chose real, regular guys, not super spiritual guys – not girly men – not weak men – and not wimpy men. Jesus chose strong men, and he persuaded them with the same message that we preach today. Those men responded the same way men have responded for over 2000 years...all in, and in many darker days, at the expense of their very life.

Real men are not perfect, and real men get into it with each other sometimes. They do that every once in awhile and that doesn't mean they need fixing...it just means they are men! Have you ever read the story of where Paul and Peter got in an argument? The Bible says that Paul said, "I withstood him to his face, and there was no small contention." Can you imagine that? But real men are able to move on, let it go, and remain friends and brothers.

I can't stand all of the pictures churches have of the men from Bible times hanging on their walls. These pictures and paintings come from the Middle Ages, and they depict an old pale Jesus and bony David. David slew a lion and a bear! The apostles look like little, wimpy men. Where does that come from? These were 'real guys' – fishermen – hard-working men!

We falsely think that men are afraid to commit and that they're afraid of structure, but that isn't the case. Wives need to understand that while commitment might not come very quick to most men, when they finally do, it is a profound statement of love they are making, and they are just as vulnerable during that season as you are. Others say that men don't come to church because they're just not expressive. Well, no one knows better than the wife of a sports fan, that this isn't the case at all. They can get real expressive!

I'm talking about real men, ladies. Sometimes my wife Cherise will want me to go to a chick flick with her, and I go because it's important to her, and sometimes we find a real winner we both like. But I like my movies as much as anyone else; my son Drake and I like our "manly" movies. We like some killing. We like some bombs going off. We like some shooting. We like some fighting, and some underdog beating the bully and even some revenge at the end!

Church Imitating Life

I had a movie-going experience not too long ago with my wife. She wanted me to go to one that I knew would be a 'chick flick.' Even the name had 'chick flick' written all over it. That's why I loaded up with popcorn, candy, nachos, everything. I knew this was going to be a long one, and I needed something to pacify me.

As I settled into my seat and began looking around the theatre, I noticed there were lots of women, but only four other men were with their wives. I said, "Look at these men. Look at them!" They were absolutely miserable. And then it hit me. This mirrored that 1 in 5 number we talked about earlier…only 1 in 5 women have their husband with them in church. You know, if we're not careful, we'll turn church into a chick flick! Men will come only out of duty and obligation. Nothing attracts men! There's no adventure. There's no fire. There's no passion. There's no challenge. There's no conquering. It's just a chick flick, romantic and sweet.

An organization conducted a study focused on words that people associate with church. They used two very different lists of words and then asked the male and female respondents to choose which list best described the church experience. The lists are below:

List 1	List 2
Feelings	Power
Sharing	Efficiency
Love	Achievement
Communication	Skill
Support	Goal Oriented
Help	Competition
	Success

After the men and women looked at the two lists, they were asked to choose which list of words best describe their church experience. Both groups (the men and women) said that list 1 above describes "church." But the problem is that one group of words makes men come alive and the other group of words makes women come alive. List 2 makes men come alive, but for most men, that list would not describe their church experience...and so here we are with only 1 in 5 women sitting with their husband in church. It turns out that men vote with their feet.

There's a lot of singing in church, and men, in general, don't like to sing. They are very self-conscious about their voices and it's just something they don't really do in any other part of their public life. Church involves a lot of handholding, and many times, that means with other men. One time when I was traveling and speaking, I brought one of our men with me. Anthony and I were both sitting on the platform in front of thousands and thousands of people there in the audience. I was getting ready to preach. As the speaker went on and on in another language, neither one of us had any idea what was being said, but I nodded when they nodded and laughed when they laughed, just trying to be polite. I acted like I was into it because I didn't know what they were saying.

At one point the preacher said something at a time of prayer and we both thought he said, "Hold hands." Anthony reached over and grabbed my hand, so we started praying and holding hands. After a bit, I decided to take a peek around, and that's when I noticed that nobody else was holding hands but Anthony and me!

I turned to him right in the middle of the prayer and I whispered (half laughing), "I should jack you up. What are you doing?" Anthony was just as startled as I was and then we almost couldn't stop laughing. That's just not something we men are used to or are comfortable with. Why are men not attracted to church? It's not a criticism of women. It's just me being honest with you about the things that keep men from the house of God...which, for many men, means that keep them from God Himself. This is not a negative reflection on women. We just need some balance in the church.

In the psyche of a man, the concept of the church ("The bride of Christ") just doesn't quite compute and neither do some of the songs we sing. Little by little, we see men leaving the church in droves. They lose interest because there was no message that challenged them. There was no message that motivated them. There was no message that caused them to feel like they were a part and belonged.

Risk and adventure were taken out of the church, and suddenly, it was all about safety and security. The word "sanctuary" comes from the word "security." Women want security and safety. Men want risk and adventure, and when the church becomes just a little safe place, we lose their interest. That's where tradition comes from. We don't want to change anything. We want it safe, and we want it secure. The church then becomes traditional, the guys get bored, and they stop coming!

We tell our men, "If you get saved, you're going to go to Heaven." Men are even afraid to go to Heaven because what we've taught them is wrong. We've taught them that when you get to Heaven, you are going to sit on a cloud with some little fat babies with angel's wings and play a harp. Why would a man want to do that for eternity?

We tell them, "Gentlemen, we're going to get a harp and we're going to sit up there and just play that harp for Jesus. For the first ten thousand years, we're going to sing Hallelujah. Reach over and join the man's hand next to you and let's sing a song." The average man simply cannot relate.

But on the other hand, the Islamic religion teaches that "If you go to heaven, the first thing a man gets is 72 virgins!" That's why they blow themselves up! They think they're going to get 72 virgins. (The thing is, they might find out it's a 72-year-old virgin!) This thing's warped. This is just not appealing because men don't get that. That's not what the Bible teaches about the Kingdom of God. Jesus preached about rewards that would be given. He said, *"If you're faithful in this life, you will rule over cities. You will serve and rule nations with a rod of iron."* That beats playing a harp for fat babies any day!!

"Jesus preached the Kingdom of Heaven suffers violence and the violent take it by force." Faith means guts! Faith means, "Walking on the water." Faith means, "Slaying a giant with a small stone." Faith means fearlessness! And the Lord says, "Wake up the mighty men—we need you. Your family needs you and you have a place and a role to play in the 21ˢᵗ century church!"

Jesus never tried to win the children so He could win the family. I thank God for our children's ministry, and as far as I'm concerned, it's the greatest in the nation. Our Kidpak program is amazing and phenomenal! But you know what? We do that because of the plague of the fatherless. We make no bones about it; we try to reach families through the children. But Jesus' ministry didn't do that. **Jesus knew that "If I reach the men, I reach the family."**

You see, in families where only the woman serves God, 17% of the time the children will follow in that faith, but in the families where the man serves God with the wife, 93% of the time, the family and children will follow Jesus Christ. That's why Joshua said, "As for me and my house, we will serve the Lord!" – "I'm not taking votes" – "I'm not asking for a poll" – **"I'm telling you that "me and my house, we will serve the Lord."**

Wives

Wives, the way you treat your man at home will have a lot to do with whether or not your man comes with you to church. The Bible says that "a foolish woman tears down her own house." Every wife and mother should write that one on your refrigerator. A foolish woman also tears down her own husband; she says things to him like "You good for nothing" – "you don't do this" – "you don't..." The Bible says, Mom, that you're a fool if you call your children stupid. You're a fool if you don't build up your husband. You're a foolish woman if you tear down your own home and your own family.

If you have a husband who went to church with you this week, you have something that four out of five women nationally don't have. You are one out of five that do. If he comes to church with you – if he loves you – if he loves those children – if he's faithful to you - My God! You need to get off his case and leave that man alone! You may say, "Well, I want him to be more spiritual. I just think he should be more like this or that." Remember: **"A foolish woman tears down her own house."** If he goes with you to church, you should be shouting happily. You should be praying, "Thank You Jesus for this good man."

"If he would only do this, if he would only do that." Lady, you should have married the Pope! None of us are that holy. None of us are walking around in white robes. At some point, you need to be thankful that you have a Mighty Man of God who at least cares enough to come to church with you.

Men, if you are a man reading this, I just went to bat for you. Now you need to man-up and get yourself to church. There is too much at stake for your marriage, for your children, and for your future to just brush this off and go be your old selfish self. There is a war raging, and we need you in that battle. Fight for your family. Fight for your faith. It's time for the mighty men of God to rise up.

Wives, if your man worships with you, then ask yourself: when was the last time you stopped and said, "I'm thankful for you? You're a good man." Sometimes, you can just put him down and focus on everything else. When's the last time you said, "You're a good man?" Cut the guy some slack. Let him watch his ballgame without getting your vacuum cleaner out. Bam! "When are you going to cut the grass?" Give him a break. Let him watch his ballgame. Order him a pizza. Go out with your girlfriends and get a coffee. Leave that man alone!

If we set the standard so high that men feel like they can never achieve it, well, they won't try. They can never be the model dad that's presented at church. "I could never be that holy" – "I could never be that good," he thinks. If we keep setting that bar so high that every time they come in here they're made to feel like they're a failure, then we are the one failing to show them who God really is and what He thinks about them.

We need to encourage our men. We need to encourage our teenage sons, and moms need to understand that the way they allow their sons to interact with them will be the way that they interact with and treat their wives. We need to correct when necessary but, more importantly, we need to encourage young men in the Lord and in the business of God. We've got to stop putting them down and telling them everything that is wrong with them! You keep them in church, and God will deal with them about everything, but your nagging is sure to keep them away.

A Band of Men

Wake up the mighty men. The church has been without one of our greatest resources, mighty men, for far too long! The mentality of the church and what we communicate must change. God designed the church to attract men; not repel them. Wake Up The Mighty Men. Wake them up! Challenge them! Call them to commitment!

I Samuel, Chapter 10 verse 26 is one of my favorite scriptures. "And Saul also went home to Gibeah; and there went with him a band of men, whose hearts God had touched."

"A band of men." I remember the first time I read that. Something in me cried out, "Oh God, give me a band of men, in my church, whose hearts God has touched." Because if a man's heart has been touched by God, he'll be a better husband – he'll be a better father – he'll be a better dad - he'll be a better leader – he'll be a better provider. More than anything else, we need men whose hearts have been touched by God.

Encounter

Have you been fast with your words and slow with your actions? Have you said much and listened little? It's hard to take back the sting of name-calling and insults. But it's equally hard to take back prolonged periods of silence. Right now, ask God to show you what you can change in the way you talk to your spouse.

Engage

Think of five ways you can encourage your spouse this week. Write them below.

Real Solutions

My wife is a good woman and a good Christian, but I don't feel like we are the same as we were when we got married. I am the same, but the more she and the kids get involved in church, the more she is changing. I feel like it's hurting our relationship. I am not as into church as she is. She would like me to go more but Sunday is my main day off and I don't like filling it up with activity and more obligations, and I am too tired to go to mid-week church stuff. It feels like I am losing her. She doesn't say anything, but I know that she knows it's different. Why is this and what should I do?

What you are experiencing is real. Many couples in the church today are becoming unequally yoked because the wife is growing in her faith and the man is not; she's at church and he isn't; she's at women's Bible study and he isn't; she is serving and he isn't; she's in a small group and he isn't.

She is gaining a spiritual maturity that the man is missing which is creating a division. She is learning what a Godly man looks like and the husband isn't even trying to grow. I'll bet if the men reading this book were honest, a good percentage of them would say they are reading it because their wife is making them do it.

The bottom line is men have to step up and decide if they want a relationship with God or not. Men have to plug into their relationship with Jesus in tangible ways and begin to build a world around people and places that will feed his soul. In this case, I don't think the woman is being a fanatic. She has just experienced something that provides incredible meaning and purpose. Why resist this? My challenge to you is this: Just give it three months. Plug in to your church by being there and get involved wherever you feel comfortable. See if the God of the universe doesn't begin to tug at your heart strings as He calls you to a higher purpose than you have ever imagined.

Sir, you KNOW that you were made for more than you are today. Plug in and allow the Lord to show you His awesome and amazing plan for your life.

CHAPTER 6

The Band of Men Whose Heart God Has Touched

> "
> All men dream, but not equally. Those who dream by night in the dusty recesses of their minds, wake in the day to find that it was vanity: but the dreamers of the day are dangerous men, for they may act on their dreams with open eyes, to make them possible. —T. E. Lawrence
> "

Charles Spurgeon is a famous theologian whom I love to study. His heart was touched by God, and he began to preach. As a result, God used him to literally shake all of Europe. Billy Sunday was a professional baseball player at the turn of the last century. But once his heart was touched by God, he began to preach, and his preaching would go on to change the world. He was flamboyant and charismatic and attracted large crowds. History tells us he would roll up his sleeves and say, "Come on smutty face" – acting like he was fighting Satan himself – "Come on smutty face devil. We're going to go a few rounds!" Men would come by the thousands to hear him preach because "one man's heart got touched by God." He was a man's man, but a deeply spiritual and devoted man as well. We need both!

Another man that was touched by God was a very famous physician named David Livingston, who lived in England in the 19th century. Livingston was a man who exchanged fame and fortune in the medical field to be a medical missionary, evangelist, an international scientific investigator as well as an anti-slavery crusader. He was a household name in England because of the discoveries that he had made in medicine. One day he heard a missionary talk about how, on a tour through Africa, he could see a thousand campfires burning in villages, villages that he knew had never heard the name of Jesus.

"Do not be afraid of their faces,

For I am with you to deliver you," says the Lord.

Then the Lord put forth His hand and touched my mouth, and the Lord said to me:

"Behold, I have put My words in your mouth.

See, I have this day set you over the nations and over the kingdoms,

To root out and to pull down,

To destroy and to throw down,

To build and to plant" (Jeremiah 1:8-10).

As he listened, Livingston felt the touch of God come upon him, so much so that he could hardly stand it. God touched that physician's heart that day and Livingston said, "I'm going to leave everything and preach the Gospel to those Africans." After some time of preparation for the trip and to get his affairs in order, he left for Africa. Many years later, Livingston's diary was found. It talks about all that he encountered on his trip. He encountered wild animals, was attacked by lions and savages, and fell ill from all kinds of diseases. He went through many medical maladies and was even bitten by a snake. Everything you can imagine, he went through it, and more. You should read his story some time.

For 40 years, the people of England didn't hear anything from Livingston except reports of churches that had been established in the forest, in the most remote parts of Africa. Finally, after about 40 years, a newspaper journalist by the name of Stanley said, "I'm going to go find Livingston and see how the story ends." Stanley searched for over a year in Africa before he finally found Livingston in a remote village in the Congo, deep in the heart of Africa.

When he got there, he said, "Livingston had wasted down to nothing. He had a fever and had numerous viruses in his body from insects that had bitten him." Stanley begged him, saying, "Come home with me. You've done a great work. You'll be celebrated as a national hero. All of England wants to welcome you home. Come home with me." Livingston refused. He refused to take one single step back from the call God had on his life. That's what real men do!

After unsuccessful attempts to get Livingston to go home with him, Stanley goes on to record that Livingston wrote the following in his diary, "I pray that God will take me home one year from now." Within a few months, he died of yellow fever. When they found him, he was on his knees in the prayer position.

When the king of England heard about his death, he sent armed guards and soldiers to retrieve the body. The natives tried to resist them, but they couldn't because of the weapons. The natives knew it would be futile to try to prevent the soldiers from taking Livingston's body. When the soldiers finally found Livingston's body and prepared to take it back to London, they discovered that his chest had been cut open. The natives had torn his heart out and buried it in the soil of Africa because they loved him so much. They said, **"You can take his body, but his heart belongs to Africa."** That was a people whose heart had been touched by a man whose heart had been touched by Jesus.

Livingston's body was buried in Westminster Abbey Church, in the heart of London, the place where England buried their nation's heroes. This hero of the faith, David Livingston, lies alongside kings and royalty to this very day.

What would happen if every man reading this book would say, "God, make me a part of **'the band of men whose heart God has touched.'"** What would happen if every wife would pray that the Lord would touch her husband's heart? How long has it been since God touched your heart? How long has it been since God touched you with a fresh touch? When He touches my heart, I can tell. When I am carnal, I can tell. When I'm not what I should be I know it, and I feel the conviction of the Holy Spirit. I can see things start going wrong in my family, and it all comes back to me. If I'll just let God touch my heart, He'll help me with my home – He'll help me with my family – He'll help me with this ministry. He will help you with YOUR family. He will help you with YOUR home. He will show you YOUR purpose.

I often pray, **"Oh God, give us 'men whose hearts have been touched by God.'** Make me a man **'whose heart has been touched by God!'"**

> *And it happened when He was in a certain city, that behold,*
>
> *a man who was full of leprosy saw Jesus;*
>
> *and he fell on his face and implored Him, saying,*
>
> *"Lord, if You are willing, You can make me clean."*

Then He put out His hand and touched him, saying,

"I am willing; be cleansed." Immediately the leprosy left him (Luke 5:12-16).

Wake up the mighty men. I want you to read this powerful excerpt from an article. It's about James Dobson, the man who founded Focus on the Family, one of the largest and most powerful ministries to families on the earth today:

A little known but classic example may be seen in the life of this Christian family leader, Dr. James Dobson. His granddaddy, a godly pastor, carried an unusually strong burden for his earthly family and spent weeks in prayer fasting for them. Once when he emerged from his time with God, he announced that God had promised him that every one of his children and grandchildren would faithfully serve the Lord in full time Christian work some day.

He said God had promised this to him. As time went on, and as those children grew up, this proved to be true. Every one of his immediate family members became a pastor, or a missionary, or married to a pastor or missionary. It was also true with the dozen grandchildren of the third generation with only one exception: James Dobson.

James did not feel led into full time Christian work, nor did he want to become an ordained minister, yet he could not escape the faith of obedience of his godly grandfather. Is it not a remarkable blessing how God has used this dedicated Christian layman to minister to all the families of America, and the world and especially the church? Dr. Dobson's grandfather had a burden for his own earthly family, and God turned that concern into a blessing for all the families of the earth. The James Dobson radio ministry has spanned the globe. His books have sold millions of copies, building families and marriages. Why? **Because one grandfather had a heart that "was touched by God!"**

Every one of those children - every one of the grandchildren - served God. It can happen for you. I'm telling you, the devil is after our families, and he's after us men. Sometimes I just feel like I don't know how to do this. I have five children and a wife. I have all this stuff going on, and sometimes I just feel like I want to run away. Sometimes I just feel like I want to walk out and say, "God, I don't know what to do! I can't take it anymore." It's in those times that I've learned I must get alone with God and have a heart that's been touched by God. And so do you. All I know is that if He touches my heart, miracles happen. If I get right with God, my family gets right – if I get right with God, my marriage gets right - if I get right with God, the ministry gets right. **"We need God to touch our hearts!"** Wake up the mighty men!

Maybe you are reading this book right now and you would say, "Jentezen, I'm not the man I should be. I have sin in my life. I have secret things going on. I have issues that nobody knows about. I have things in my life that I know are separating me from God. I'm a backslider." Trust me when I say that the Lord knows all that, and you are the reason He sent His Son. I am the reason He sent His son. God forgives. He has a purpose for you in the Kingdom.

Don't say, "Well, one day I'm going to give my whole heart and my WHOLE life to God." You don't know that there will even be a tomorrow. You don't know how long you have with that family. You'd better make every day count. Give your life to Jesus right now. Ask for Jesus to touch you right now, and He will. All that is needed is a willing heart to change and these three simple words, "Touch me, Jesus." One touch is all it takes.

Shackled by a heavy burden,

'neath a load of guilt and shame;

Then the hand of Jesus touched me,

And now I am no longer the same.

He touched me, O, He touched me,

And O, the joy that floods my soul.

Something happened, and now I know,

 He touched me and made me whole.

Since I met this blessed Savior,

Since He cleansed and made me whole;

I will never cease to praise Him,

I'll shout it while eternity rolls.

He touched me, O, He touched me,

And O, the joy that floods my soul.

Something happened, and now I know,

He touched me and made me whole.

—He Touched Me by Bill Gaither

Encounter

This moment is just for you and God. Getting your heart in line vertically will lead to better relationships horizontally. Reflect below on what you hear the Lord saying to you about these alignments of the heart:

....

....

....

....

....

....

....

Engage

Pray the Lord's prayer out loud and take a moment to allow the Lord to speak to your heart:

Our Father in heaven, hallowed be your name, your kingdom come, your will be done, on earth as it is in heaven. Give us today our daily bread. And forgive us our debts, as we also have forgiven our debtors. And lead us not into temptation, but deliver us from the evil one (Matthew 6:9-13).

I struggle with pornography a little. I'm not cheating on my wife with another woman or even flirting, and I would never even consider infidelity. But sometimes I just like to take a look or maybe watch for a while. I love the Lord, and I do experience guilt, but it seems harmless. Why is this so wrong?

Let me be clear: It is wrong. It is sin. It will destroy your marriage. And if you don't stop now, little by little you will create separation in your marriage resulting in a gulf that will be very difficult to get across. One of the greatest struggles a spouse will ever go through is infidelity, and regardless of what you might think, many spouses view this as a form of infidelity. Before God, it is infidelity. And while this is an issue women struggle with as well, it is an epidemic in men. Sadly, even in the church.

Pornography's devastating effects are not always sudden and deadly, but rather little by little, it creates insensitivity in a person where the intimate embrace is exchanged for a physical sensation. This separation will never be felt as much by the man, who is more visually and physically driven, as it will for the women who seek intimacy and an emotional connection. The flesh wins . . . and the heart loses.

The greatest tragedy of the pornography issue though, isn't nearly as much about the actual sin as it is about the trust that has been violated with the spouse. Sin is covered by the blood and can be forgiven. Trust, on the other hand is an altogether different matter. That kind of damage runs deep.

If this is something you are playing with . . . stop. STOP. The sensation you experience in the highest high will NEVER be worth the damage you will cause in the very people you love most. STOP!!! Satan has you in his sights and you are falling for his deception. But like all deception, you have to understand this immutable principle: There are some things God will allow you to have in the liberty and free will He extends. But there are some things you have right now - that will some day, have YOU. And your spouse. And your children. And your testimony. And everything you hold dearest and most sacred. STOP!

If your right eye offends you PLUCK IT OUT. And if your computer offends you, GET OFF IT! If your iPhone offends you, GET RID of it. You may say, well I can't

---

live without those things. Well, then you need to either invest in restrictions you can't change or software that alerts your spouse to every website you visit. Here's what you will realize some day, and hopefully before it's too late: There are only two things you can't do without and that is your relationship to Jesus Christ and your family. So why even take one step down that road? STOP..

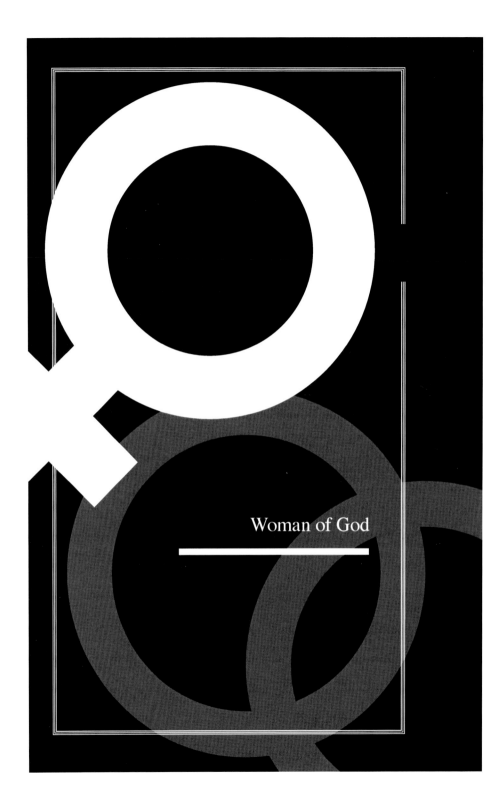

Woman of God

CHAPTER 7

Woman...As God Designed You

> "
>
> A beautiful woman delights the eye; a wise woman, the understanding; a pure one, the soul.
> —Minna Antrim
>
> "

And Adam gave names to all the cattle, and to the fowl of the air, and to every beast of the field, but for Adam, there was not found a helpmate for him. And the Lord God caused a deep sleep to fall upon Adam, and he slept, and He took one of his ribs, and closed up the flesh instead thereof.

And the rib, which the Lord God had taken from man, made He a woman, and brought her unto the man. And Adam said, "This is now bone of my bone, and flesh of my flesh, she shall be called Woman, because she was taken out of Man."

Therefore shall a man leave his father and his mother, and shall cleave unto his wife, and they shall be one flesh. And they were both naked, and they were not ashamed (Genesis 2:20-25).

"Adam called her Woman." The simple title for this chapter is one word: **Woman.** The Bible says that God made Adam (man) from the dust of the earth. The literal word means topsoil. In other words, he was to be fruitful and productive. God made Adam and everything else that existed on this planet by non-living material – dust!

But when it came time for the creation of woman, God did it in a very different way. He put Adam to sleep. He opened up the side of Adam, reached in, pulled a rib out, and constructed woman. He created woman out of a living thing. Adam and all of the animals, the stars, the moon, the sun, everything that God created was created out of nonliving material. But when it came to woman, God made her from a living being, a living organism. He reached in and pulled her out from Adam and formed a life from life.

Why was the creation of a woman different from any and every other creation on the planet? To the women reading this book, I want you to understand that you are special. You did not come from dirt; you came from life. God chose to make you from living material because God knew that you would become the doorway of life. Every life that comes into this planet must pass through the womb of a woman. Even God, when He decided to send His Son, circumvented man. He didn't need man to produce a Savior named Jesus. He went around man, and through that woman, because she is the doorway of life. Women in the 21st century need to embrace a profound truth. You need to know that God has you here for a great purpose, a purpose that was instituted in the creation story of Genesis.

It Is Very Good

Follow through the steps of creation and you'll notice that every time God created something, He said, 'It is good." When God got to the sixth day, after He had created everything else, He created woman. And when He created her, He stepped back and made a very different proclamation. Every other time, He said, "It is good," but this time, after He created woman, He said, "It is VERY good."

In Genesis, chapter 2, verses 1-3, there is a powerful revelation that women need to understand and take deep into their soul:

Thus the heavens and the earth were finished, and all the host of them.

And on the seventh day God ended his work which he had made;

and he rested on the seventh day from all his work which he had made.

And God blessed the seventh day, and sanctified it:

because that in it he had rested from all his work which God created and made.

After God created woman, the last creation, God said on the seventh day, "This is the Sabbath, and it's going to be a day of rest." It's going to be a day of calm. It's going to be a day of peace. The Sabbath is the rest day. It's not a negative, it's a positive. God put in the woman the ability to bring Sabbath-- rest, calm, peace, tranquility, serenity-- to the home. But just as she is able to bring calm and peace--Sabbath--, she also has the ability to bring a storm, and I always get far too many AMENs when I preach that, especially at Men's Meetings!

Storms and Calm

It's interesting that, initially, hurricanes were always named after women! For many years, hurricanes and other tropical storms bore only girls' names. There were never any named Tom or Jack; it was always a woman's name. In that era when political correctness had never been heard of, the exclusively male meteorological community in the USA considered female names appropriate for such unpredictable and dangerous phenomena. In the 1970s the growing numbers of female meteorologists began to object to such a sexist practice, and from 1978 onward girls' and boys' names alternated. Even recent well-known hurricanes and tropical storms are named after women such as Isabel (2003), Bonnie (2004), Katrina (2005), Florence (2006), Melissa (2007), Bertha (2008), Sandy (2012).

There's a lesson in that. The reason is that God was and is wanting women to understand the powerful ability He has placed inside of each and every woman! She can bring the hurricane and chaos, or she can bring the Sabbath (the peace, the calm, the serenity of God) upon her household. Have you ever heard the saying *"If Mama ain't happy; ain't nobody happy?"* That's the truth!

Even the Jews understood that. In the Jewish home, the Sabbath could not be brought in by a man. It was the woman that beckoned and ushered in the Sabbath; it was she who asked the peace of God to come into her home. Even to this day in Jewish homes, it is the woman who places the candle in the holder, and it's the woman who lights the candle. It is the woman who has to pray the prayer of the Sabbath.

It's compelling when you understand that God has given something powerful to every woman. It is the ability to cause either a great peace (a Sabbath, great rest, contentment, and calm) or a hurricane of chaos in your home. That's why the Scripture teaches about the role of women. If there is going to be rest in a home, then women have the capacity to call it into their homes.

Proverbs reveals just how powerful this storm aspect inside of every woman can be:

Every wise woman builds her house, but a foolish woman tears it down with her own hands (Proverbs 14:1 Amplified).

It's better to be on the housetop, in all kinds of weather, than in a house shared with a nagging, quarrelsome and faultfinding woman (Proverbs 21:9 Amplified).

A quarrelsome wife is like a constant dripping on a rainy day; restraining her is like restraining the wind or grasping oil with the hand (Proverbs 27:15-16).

"A continual dripping" is drip, drip, drip, which is like water torture...drip, drip, drip. This is an actual torture tactic that some countries have used to drive their enemies insane. They would tie up a prisoner and drip, drip, drip a drop of water on his head until he went insane. In these Scriptures, God is saying to you, ladies, that you have two choices; you can either become this constant "drip," or you can usher in "the Sabbath" into your home.

You can complain – drip, drip, drip. You are constantly negative – drip, drip, drip. You can tear down your children and tear down your husband – drip, drip, drip. Or, you can build up your children. You can build up your house. You can usher in the peace, or you can usher in the storm. It's up to you.

A Godly Tenacity

God wants you to turn all this potential into a positive. He doesn't want you to turn it on your family, or turn it on people who are getting on your nerves. He wants you to turn it on the devil. He wants you to use it against demonic forces. He wants you to use it in prayer – drip, drip, drip. . You must keep praying for your husband – keep praying for those children, drip, drip, drip. That's torturing the enemy. You just keep praising – you just keep teaching – you just keep encouraging – you just keep building up - drip; drip, drip. It tortures and it breaks the power of the enemy and it ushers the Sabbath into your home.

When God created woman, nothing was missing. Everything was complete. Everything was in order. When He made her, God put something in woman that needs to have order. A woman is not comfortable when there is not order. That's why when the house is not in order – when the kids' rooms are not in order – when the house looks like a trial run for the battle of Armageddon, she is not going to usher in a calm Sabbath. She is going to have a problem because God made her that way.

Taken From the Rib

Another concept we must never lose sight of is that woman was taken from the rib of man. The rib has the primary purpose of protecting the heart, which is the vital organ of the body. It's placed in perfect position as to be near the heart, to feel the heartbeat. That means there is a natural inclination in women to need to feel the heartbeat of their husbands. You cannot be distant and your wife be satisfied. She's just being the rib, and the rib is close to the heart and must feel the heart. There's a tendency in her to probe – "How do you feel about this?" – "How do you feel about that?" What is she doing? She's searching for a heartbeat, and when she can't hear it, she is going to build one!

Men like to keep everything inside, especially when we are going through trying times. But a woman feels the need to hear from you, to find out what's going on with your heart. This can be difficult for the man, especially if he's trying to watch the NBA playoffs or just about any sporting event. But you have to understand that God created her that way. She's not just going to go about her business around the house and let you read your paper. She's got to feel your heartbeat! She needs to hear where you are; she needs to know there is life in there, life in you, and life in your marriage.

In our first few years of marriage we lived with my mother-in-law, but we knew it was time for us to spread our wings and get our own home. We had saved our money, and I thought I had found the perfect house north of town. Notice that *I* thought *I* had found the perfect house. *I* loved this house. This house was just amazing to *me*. I'll never forget pulling up, getting out, and walking into this house *I* had picked out to be our first house. It needed some updates, it didn't have curtains, and the floor in the kitchen needed some work done to it, but I thought it was just cosmetic. After all, a man's home is his castle, and *I* had found *our* castle. I could just see myself in that home, and I was so excited.

We were looking it over with the real estate lady standing there and I said, "I love it. What do you think, Cherise?" Without so much as a pause or a loving glance, she said, "I'm not staying here." I said, "Excuse me?" She said, "Look at that kitchen. There are no curtains on the windows. Look at the floors. The bathroom is hideous." Turns out I needed an "I" appointment with the "I" doctor and I didn't even know "I" had a problem.

She needed order. She needed completion. She needed to feel the heartbeat, and she wasn't getting that from this house. Later we would both see that it wasn't the right house for us. Had it been up to me in that moment, we would have made a bad decision. And thank God that even though we were young, I was wise enough to know on the big decisions, surprises are NEVER wise.

In Scripture, the church is referred to as a woman. References are made to the Bride and the Bridegroom. Jesus is the Bridegroom, we are the Bride. I've often wondered why He referred to the church in the feminine gender. But when you stop and consider it, just as in the natural, the only doorway to life is through the woman, and so the doorway to spiritual life in the church is through a woman. In Ephesians 5:30-32, the apostle Paul writes:

> *For we are members of His body, of His flesh and of His bones. "For this reason a man shall leave his father and mother and be joined to his wife, and the two shall become one flesh." This is a great mystery, but I speak concerning Christ and the church* (NKJV).

He's trying to get us to understand that, as it is with a husband and a wife, so it is with Christ and the church. God isn't modeling it after men. You're so important, women, that He modeled the church after you. I Peter 3:4 says,

> *"but let it be [the inner beauty of] the hidden person of the heart, with the imperishable quality and unfading charm of a gentle and peaceful spirit, one that is calm and self-controlled, not overanxious, but serene and spiritually mature which is very precious in the sight of God"* (I Peter 3:4).

There it is – the Sabbath! *"A gentle and a peaceful spirit"* which is not anxious or worked up. It is very precious in the sight of God. God loves to see a gentle and peaceful spirit that is not giving way to hysterical fears or letting anxiety unnerve you.

One of Satan's great battle plans is to stir up women in their homes. Satan wants to work women up into hysteria. He wants to use anxiety to unnerve you. He doesn't want you to stand and call the Sabbath "the peace."

Snakes

I thought about how snakes have always been used to represent the things that Satan sends. Snakes pop up in your life – when something's wrong with your children – when there's an attack, physically, against your body – and you need to be ready for the attack when the snake comes into your life.

While I do not want to generalize, it's so easy to go into hysteria and to become upset and to fall to pieces. But God's plan has a right reaction. You're not supposed to go into a hurricane of chaos when challenges come against you. When 'snakes' from the devil show up in your life trying to destroy your family or trying to destroy your marriage, don't give way to the anxiety that unnerves you and causes you to go into hysteria. Stay calm! Call the "Sabbath" in! God put in you the ability to call the "Sabbath" into that situation – the rest – the calm – the peace.

You have to choose! Proverbs 18 has several verses that apply to this concept:

The words of a man's (or woman's) mouth are deep waters, but the fountain of wisdom is a babbling brook"(v 4).

A fool's lips bring strife, and his (or her) mouth invites a beating. A fool's mouth is his (or her) undoing, and his (or her) lips are a snare to his (or her) soul (v 6-7).

The tongue has the power of life and death, and those who love it will eat its fruit (v 21).

Understand this: You'd better like what you're saying about your family, about your children, and about your future because you're going to eat the words you're saying. Your words will come back to you.

So many women deal with their self-image. Many women just can't quite live up to the image of the glossy model that has been photo enhanced. It's not unusual for women to look in the mirror and say, "Look at me. I can't stand my body. Look at me. I don't like my face or my weight or my hair."

I think all of this traces back to Barbie. For many women, it goes all the way back to Barbie because she is amazing and perfect! Barbie has a great figure – she's 34, 24, 34 – and has a Ken in her life. Isn't that the perfect image? Barbie has a Corvette and lives in a Malibu mansion. Barbie is the image to which every woman is supposed to measure up. If you don't have what Barbie has and if you don't look like Barbie looks, then you're not good enough.

Contrast that nonsense with what God is showing you…about YOU. God would say to you, "You're made in My image and in My likeness. I like you just the way you are. I like your lips. I like your nose and your height and your eyes and everything about you. In fact, not only do I like you just the way you are…every inch inside and out was My idea….YOU were My idea."

God made you like you are. There's a freedom in accepting the fact that you don't have to be anybody but yourself. God has your life planned out. He has everything that you need for you to be the woman He created you to be!

There are kids starving themselves, and young girls that are anorexic or bulimic, and many times that comes to a fatal end. We have kids with eating disorders because they're swallowing the lie of a false image of the world they live in and digesting it deep into their soul and psyche.

I want every woman to get just this simple little lesson out of this chapter. Number one, you are the doorway of life for your family. You are the doorway to spiritual life to your marriage and to your whole family. You have the power to "call the calm," the Sabbath, into your home, into your marriage, and into your family. You can beckon "the Sabbath" in any crisis. You are the peacemaker.

You need to declare, "Thank You, Lord for how You made me. I'm going to quit 'woman wishing' because it doesn't do any good!" I want you to get so full of faith that you say, "I know I look good in my high heels and my Louis Vuitton purse. But devil, don't you mistake all this silk for something it isn't, because under the silk, I have a sword! I know how to take you out. And I have a shield and I know how to 'call in the calm.' I'll use my hurricane power against you! Don't touch my children. I know how to anoint every door knob. I know how to walk in the bedroom and pray over the beds of my children. I know how to confess the blessing of God over my marriage and over my family!"

Life is too short to go through it upset all the time. Enjoy life. Enjoy your family. Enjoy your husband. Enjoy where you are. Know that God has a plan. He made you and He knows what is best for you, and He's working His will! Call on the peace of God. You are literally and figuratively the doorway to spiritual life. Come out of that self-made pit of false-image and that pit of anxiety. Give birth to praise. Give birth to life.

Encounter

Earlier in the book, we discussed the importance of atmosphere. We hold the power to set the atmosphere. As believers, we don't have to accept the temperature of a situation, we can control the thermostat! We can combat lies with truth, despair with hope, mourning with joy, anxiety with peace; through Christ, we hold the keys. Journal below how you hear the Lord talking to you about the atmosphere you have been setting.

Engage

Ask God to help you identify attitudes in your marriage that need to change, and journal about what you will be doing differently. Ask the Lord to show you how you can be the catalyst of change.

As a wife, what is the best way to submit to your husband even if you feel he is being disrespectful, unloving and critical toward you (especially during arguments)? How do you maintain healthy, safe environments, respect for yourself, and healthy self-esteem while still respecting him?

There are different kinds of abuse, physical and emotional. Where there is physical abuse you need to tell someone and even report it to the authorities. Any pastor that tells you to stick in there and get beat up needs to resign. This doesn't mean to divorce right away, but it means your safety and the safety of your children are the first priority.

But what you have described is more of a mentally abusive situation. And nine times out of ten, it is not nearly as much about you as the low self-esteem and insecurity of the spouse. People think bullies are confident arrogant people when in actuality they are very small insecure people who need to feel bigger.

Strength in your own walk with Jesus will bring you greater levels of confidence and those darts from the enemy through your spouse's mouth will just bounce right off because a lie cannot live . . . and you are a child of God.

How do you maintain healthy and safe environments? First of all, physical abuse will not be tolerated. Secondly, target your prayers not so much on how to endure, but rather on that small person who is lashing out from a very dark place.

There is a great book called Boundaries In Marriage by Henry Cloud and David Townsend—a bestseller. Their book will walk you through the very things you are going through. You need to arm yourself with strategies and knowledge to have the wisdom for your situation.

CHAPTER 8

Discerning Women

> ❝
> If you want something said, ask a man; if you want something done, ask a woman.
> —Margaret Thatcher
> ❞

Throughout scripture, women have had extraordinary discernment about the Body of Christ. Women were last at the Cross, refusing to believe that was the end of it all. Women were first at the tomb, and women were present in the Upper Room. After Jesus died on the Cross, the Bible says, the men went fishing, but the women said, "We're going to anoint His body."

In the book of Exodus, Pharaoh was so paranoid about someone rising up from the Hebrew slaves that he set out to kill all the male children under two. In this very dark time for the Hebrews, it was the midwives that stepped in and interceded. In the first chapter of Exodus, the Bible says that Pharaoh lodged a complaint about the midwives. The Israelites were reproducing so quickly that Pharaoh commanded that the midwives kill all the babies as they were being born. But the Bible says that the midwives couldn't get to them fast enough because the woman were having babies at such a rapid rate. And it was a midwife that saved the life of Moses, the very bloodline of Jesus.

Then the king of Egypt spoke to the Hebrew midwives, of whom the name of one was Shiphrah and the name of the other Puah; and he said, "When you do the duties of a midwife for the Hebrew women, and see them on the birth stools, if it is a son, then you shall kill him; but if it is a daughter, then she shall live." But the midwives feared God, and did not do as the king of Egypt commanded them, but saved the male children alive. So the king of Egypt called for the midwives and said to them, "Why have you done this thing, and saved the male children alive?"

And the midwives said to Pharaoh, "Because the Hebrew women are not like the Egyptian women; for they are lively and give birth before the midwives come to them" (Exodus 1:15-19).

Lively Women

Pharaoh called in the midwives and said, *"What's going on here!? These women keep putting out children and I told you to kill the babies."* The Bible says the midwives responded, "We're sorry, Pharaoh, but the Hebrew women are more lively than the Egyptian women." In the 21st century that's like saying, "There's always life when a group of godly women get together!" Godly women should be more lively than the women of "Egypt," which is a type and shadow of modern day society. There's life when women get together. The scripture says that they were bringing children to birth in the middle of "Egypt." The Egyptian culture wanted to kill the children, but these women somehow had the ability to bring children to birth and keep them alive even though they were in the midst of an Egyptian culture that did all it could to kill them.

I believe that God is looking for lively, spiritual "Hebrew" women that will bring forth godly children in the middle of an "Egyptian" culture. We live in a culture that is coming after our children to destroy them with sexual immorality, drugs, and alcohol, but if God can find some lively women, He will use them. He will use YOU to be the difference between victory and defeat.

Lively women have lively prayer lives and lively praise lives and lively consecration unto God. The scripture says that these lively women were bringing forth children even though the enemy was there trying to kill them. Because of wise and discerning women in the form of midwives, they brought forth a generation of male Hebrews that would have been otherwise slaughtered.

The Discerning Prayer of a Woman

I think of Hannah and her great cry to the Lord asking for a son. It wasn't so much that she asked for a son, which would have been a common prayer for women in that day, but Hannah understood that she had to have a Samuel. She had discernment. Something about her walked around grieving saying, "I must have a male child because Israel needs a prophet." Her husband didn't understand it. Her husband didn't detect it.

Hannah's husband said to her on one occasion when she was grieving because she could not get pregnant, "I should be better to you than a thousand sons." But she said,

"No, I must bring forth a son." Even the priest didn't discern what she did. The Bible says, "She went to the temple and acted like a drunk woman. Weeping and sobbing and crying, saying, 'Give me a child', and Eli rebuked her and said, 'What are you doing drunk in this temple?'" She knew something that neither the priest nor her husband could figure out. She had insight and an overwhelming desire to give birth to something extraordinary.

The Calming Effect of a Woman

In Genesis Chapter 33, the Lord showed me something about women that maybe you've never seen before, but I want you to grasp this. Remember that Jacob tricked his blind father into giving him the birthright of his brother Esau. This enraged Esau and brought a bitter divide between the brothers for a very long time, and Esau vowed revenge. Some time later, Jacob experienced an encounter with God that would change everything, including his name since his name was changed from Jacob to Israel.

Fast forward many years, and Jacob learns that Esau is coming toward him with four hundred soldiers. From every report, Esau is angry and he has fire in his eyes. He's coming to kill his brother. Esau was planning to destroy Jacob's family because Jacob had stolen the birthright that was meant for HIS children's inheritance. Jacob believed Esau was coming, not only to kill Jacob, but to kill his wife, to kill his children, and to kill all of those that were of the household of Jacob. That's how angry Esau had been. But the closer Esau got to the place where Jacob was, the more his disposition changed.

Then Jacob looked up, and saw Esau coming with four hundred men. So he divided the children among Leah and Rachel and the two maids. He put the maids and their children in front, Leah and her children after them, and Rachel and Joseph last of all. Then Jacob crossed over [the stream] ahead of them and bowed himself to the ground seven times [bowing and moving forward each time], until he approached his brother.

But Esau ran to meet him and embraced him, and hugged his neck and kissed him, and they wept [for joy]. Esau looked up and saw the women and the children, and said, "Who are these with you?" So Jacob replied, "They are the children whom God has graciously given your servant." Then the maids approached with their children, and they bowed down. Leah also approached with her children, and they bowed down. Afterward Joseph and Rachel approached, and they bowed down. Esau asked, "What do you mean by all this company which I have met?" And he answered, "[These are] to find favor in the sight of my lord."But Esau said, "I have plenty, my brother; keep what you have for yourself" (Genesis 33:1-8).

You may be asking yourself, "What has this to do with me today?" This story represents an Esau spirit coming against Jacob's family. The Bible says that Jacob sent presents and gifts to try to stop this attack on his family. But the Bible says Esau kept riding, having four hundred soldiers with him. And notice that Jacob put the women out front. He got behind the women, pushed them out into the presence of an invading force that was coming to kill the family.

When Esau saw the women, it broke his spirit and he started weeping saying, *"Who are these women?"* In other words, the women were able to do what money could not do and what men could not do. When women stepped out in front, Esau's spirit of destruction against the family was broken. When women stood out there and said, "You cannot destroy my husband, my family, my children, my house," it broke the spirit of revenge and destruction. Women have great authority and power.

Women Warriors

What if the women had been absent? What if the women hadn't stepped out there and interposed themselves between that spirit that was coming to destroy their marriage, their home and their family? It's not just up to men to get a hold of God, but I believe this is an hour when God is calling women to take their rightful place in the Kingdom of God. Esau could overcome numbers and men, but he couldn't overcome a bunch of praying women. They broke his spirit and made him weep. I can hear a demon saying, "Don't let those women get this information. Let them think that their job in life is just to look pretty and that's about it. Don't let them know that if they stand against the forces that come to destroy their home, God will not disregard their prayers."

The Love of a Discerning Woman

In the book of Luke, Jesus has dinner at the home of a Pharisee named Simon. From the context of the entire passage we find other men at the table with Jesus and the Pharisee. Also in the room, there was "A woman in the town who was a sinner." The passage goes on to say that she heard that Jesus was going to be at this house and she found a way to get in.

One of the Pharisees asked Jesus to eat with him, and He went into the Pharisee's house [in the region of Galilee] and reclined at the table. Now there was a woman in the city who was [known as] a [a]sinner; and [b]when she found out that He was reclining at the table in the Pharisee's house, she brought an alabaster vial of perfume; and standing behind Him at His feet, weeping, she began wetting His feet with her tears, and wiped them with the hair of her head, and [respectfully] kissed His feet [as an act signifying both affection and submission] and [c]anointed them with the perfume. Now when [Simon] the Pharisee who had invited Him saw this, he said to himself, "If this Man were a prophet He would know who and what sort of woman this is who is touching Him, that she is a [notorious] sinner [an outcast, devoted to sin]."

Jesus, answering, said to the Pharisee, "Simon, I have something to say to you." And he replied, "Teacher, say it." "A certain moneylender had two debtors: one owed him five hundred [d]denarii, and the other fifty. When they had no means of repaying [the debts], he freely forgave them both. So which of them will love him more?" Simon answered, "The one, I take it, for whom he forgave more." Jesus said to him, "You have decided correctly."

Then turning toward the woman, He said to Simon, "Do you see this woman? I came into your house [but you failed to extend to Me the usual courtesies shown to a guest]; you gave Me no water for My feet, but she has wet My feet with her tears and wiped them with her hair [demonstrating her love]. You gave Me no [welcoming] kiss, but from the moment I came in, she has not ceased to kiss My feet. You did not [even] anoint My head with [ordinary] oil, but she has anointed My feet with [costly and rare] perfume. Therefore I say to you, her sins, which are many, are forgiven, for she loved much; but he who is forgiven little, loves little." Then He said to her, "Your sins are forgiven." Those who were reclining at the table with Him began saying among themselves, "Who is this who even forgives sins?" Jesus said to the woman, "Your faith [in Me] has saved you; go in peace [free from the distress experienced because of sin]" (Luke 7:36-50).

The presence of a woman, or the absence of a woman, makes all the difference. Jesus said, *"When I was sitting up here with all of you men, none of you came and washed my feet. None of you came and anointed me. None of you came and did one thing for me."* There was not a man present who was sensitive enough to discern what was going on.

It was just God and Adam in the Garden of Eden and the Bible says, "God looked back and He said, 'It is not good that man should be alone.'" Something was missing in creation, and that something was women. God made woman and man to be together. Ladies, according to scripture, you were God's idea.

In a similar account in scripture, just days before Jesus was betrayed and murdered on a cross, another woman washed Jesus' feet and then dried them with her hair. These acts were actually anointing Him for His burial. This was Mary in the famous Mary and

Martha story. Martha was so busy doing all the cooking and preparing while her slacker sister just sat at Jesus' feet and did nothing, or at least that's how it was seen by most in the room. In actuality, while Martha was serving, Mary was worshiping.

The thing that catches our attention about this story is that Mary understood and discerned the moment and the hour while no one else did. The men and disciples did not understand or perceive anything other than an evening with Martha and Mary for dinner. Jesus even made the statement, *"Against the day of my burial, she has done this thing."* Mary weeps while the men stand completely dull to the magnitude of the moment; they just sit and judge the character of the woman and the price of the nard.

While He was in Bethany [as a guest] at the home of Simon the leper, and reclining at the table, a woman came with an alabaster vial of very costly and precious perfume of pure nard; and she broke the vial and poured the perfume over His head. But there were some who were indignantly remarking to one another, "Why has this perfume been wasted? For this perfume might have been sold for more than three hundred denarii [a laborer's wages for almost a year], and the money given to the poor." And they scolded her. But Jesus said, "Let her alone; why are you bothering her and causing trouble? She has done a good and beautiful thing to Me. For you always have the poor with you, and whenever you wish you can do something good to them; but you will not always have Me. She has done what she could; she has anointed My body beforehand for the burial. I assure you and most solemnly say to you, wherever the good news [regarding salvation] is proclaimed throughout the world, what she has done will be told in memory of her" (Mark 14:3-9).

There was something that got a hold of her spirit when Jesus entered the room. She picked up on something no one else in the room could grasp. I am sure she must have thought, "If I don't do this now, I'm going to miss the opportunity. This is the time to do something." She had tremendous discernment for the magnitude of that moment.

Three Roles of Women

The Bible teaches three things women should bring to their home, to their family, and to the Body of Christ. **First,** godly women are **discerning. Second,** the Bible teaches that women should be **prayer warriors.** Do you know the word travail is used in regard to prayer? The word travail is the word of a woman. No man knows, on the same level, what the word travail means like a woman who has brought forth a child. The same word the Bible uses to describe travailing prayer is the same way travail is used when a woman goes into labor. She is in travail, and the scripture uses that word to describe a woman in prayer – travailing in prayer.

Not only does the Bible teach that women are to be discerning and women are to be praying, but **third,** women are to have a **servant's heart.** You see, the male ego will write checks that their consecration can't cash. But there's something about the servant heart of a woman. Ladies, don't ever lose the servant heart because it is so precious in God's eyes.

The Modern Era Outpouring

Did you know that in 1901 in Topeka, Kansas at Stone's Folly, the outpouring of the Holy Spirit took place, and this "outpouring" is the birthplace for the modern day Spirit-filled movement? The history books record that the women were praying when a young girl, Agnes Osmond, had the Holy Spirit come upon her in amazing ways. The outpouring that has been known as the latter day rain came upon this woman first.

---

out·pour·ing noun

something that streams out rapidly. Outflow, rush, flood, cascade, torrent, gush, flow

---

As news of this women's prayer meeting spread, a man named Byron Seymour was invited to a another women's prayer meeting held on Bonny Brae Street in Los Angeles, California. It was in that women's prayer meeting that Byron Seymour was filled with the Holy Spirit, and that started something called the Azusa Street Revival. God was saying that He was going to pour out His Spirit from A to Z across the U.S.A. There is still a street by that name in Los Angeles and it did not start with a man. It started with a woman in an old-fashioned prayer meeting. We're here today as a result of that outpouring that started with one woman.

Satan hates women because the first thing God said about woman was, "Out of her seed shall come one who will crush the head of the serpent." When Satan heard that, he started hating women, and he has been on the attack ever since. You know how he attacks you the most? He wants to stop you from being productive. He doesn't want you to succeed or discover your purpose or your power in the Lord. He's against women being productive in any way, shape or form, because he knows his greatest threat came through a woman.

As I write this book, I know the Lord wants me to share something very valuable with you. He said to me, "There are women that will read this book, and I want you to do something." He said, "You need to break ladies free from the bondage of self-pity." Things have happened to you in life. Your Daddy left you early. You've gone through a relationship or a marriage break up. You were abused. You were mistreated. You were hurt. You were wounded. And if you're not careful, what will happen is that you begin to take on more and more self-pity. And when you throw a pity party, the only one who shows up is the devil.

So quit. Get off your pity pot. I can't help who left you and neither can you. Be thankful for those who are still with you. Your name is written in the Book of Life. He's called you by your name and He says, *"I'm with you and I'll never leave you."* I BREAK THE SPIRIT OF SELF-PITY OFF EVERY WOMAN READING THIS BOOK IN JESUS' NAME. Stand up and God will fight for you. Stand up and you'll charge the gates of Hell and shake them off their hinges. Stand up and success will not be far from you. Stand up and your children will rise up and called you blessed. God's not through with you.

The First Women's Prayer Meeting

The first mention of a gathering of women in scripture is in Genesis 24:11 when women came to a well to draw water. Did you know that the Holy Spirit is attracted to women that gather to draw water? He has gifts and blessings that He wants to put on women, and I believe God is telling you that He has placed you near a good watering hole for women to gather together. Have you lost your shout? Are you so dry? We need some lively Hebrew women, not dead spiritual women. We need some women who are alive in their praise and alive in their passion for Jesus and alive in reading the Word of God, because our families are at stake.

You have an awesome responsibility as a woman of God. There is a special calling on a woman of God in the 21st century, and God wants to use you mightily. Pray for your husband. Pray for your children. When's the last time you prayed for your husband? When's the last time you interceded for every one of your children and you stood between them and fires of destruction? I believe, if we could see in the spirit, there are Esaus that are coming to destroy homes and families. Women can stand for their marriages and for their families and break the power of that spirit. A home-wrecking force can be broken through the power of a godly woman who has a discerning spirit.

Your Finest Hour

We are in an hour when God is ready to visit and anoint women in the Body of Christ like never before and for women to perform powerful acts of service. You'd better get a spiritual broom and sweep some things out of your house. You'd better find a prayer place and understand that there's an Esau spirit that hates your family, a home wrecking spirit that wants your husband---that wants your children---that wants to get your daughter pregnant---that wants to mess up your life and the future of your children. You have to stand there and say, "God make me the woman you've called me to be." Begin to ask God in this critical hour.

Understand that you cannot play games. You cannot have a mediocre spiritual walk with God. You'd better be a lively Hebrew woman. If you're going to raise children in an Egyptian culture, you'd better have a prayer life that is alive. You must make sure that you stick with the Bible. This book is the standard and goes against so much of what today's culture is telling you to do. Ask God to make you a lively Hebrew woman. Say, "God don't let me die spiritually. Don't let my prayer life die. Don't let my praise die. Don't let my worship die. Don't let my consecration wane. I want to be lively like those midwives. Lord give me joy and make me lively in every area of my life and make me lively in my marriage."

Encounter

We see the Mary and Martha illustration which paints a vivid picture of modern day society. We work, work, work to make things perfect, overlooking the importance of simply being with one another. The most important thing you can do in your relationship is stop and just be. What is the Lord saying to you about this?

Engage

How can you be more intentional about letting your spouse know how important they are to you and how can your relationship grow in regard to being together and being fully present in the relationship?

How does a husband or wife deal with a deep desire to make love with their spouse, but the spouse has no desire whatsoever? We are both Christians with no illnesses.

I think the first thing you have to consider is, is this how they were at the beginning of the marriage or did it change at some point? A low sex drive is a physiological reality for many people and it has nothing to do with love for their partner, which can still be very strong. The bigger issue is whether the person with the low sex drive is willing to go halfway and explore medical options that can have positive effects. There are many medical programs now such as the Boston Institute that have ways to help this dramatically. And, as they say for everything else . . . there's a pill for that!

A good counselor would be able to help you identify whether it's a physiological issue or some other issue that is more about the relationship. Make an appointment right away and begin to explore your options. Marriage was never meant to be the graveyard of desire.

Scripture is clear:

Do not deprive each other except perhaps by mutual consent and for a time, so that you may devote yourselves to prayer. Then come together again so that Satan will not tempt you because of your lack of self-control. I Corinthians 7:5

Section
03

Seasoned with Salt

CHAPTER 9

An Extraordinary Covenant

"

"After the chills and fever of love, how nice is the 98.6 degrees of marriage." —Mignon McLaughlin

"

There are two major covenants of the Bible. There's "The Blood Covenant" and "The Salt Covenant." The Blood Covenant has to do with our redemption. It's how we are saved, by the blood of the sacrifice of Jesus Christ. Its origins are found as early as the book of Genesis: *"And the Lord made garments of skin for Adam and his wife and clothed them"* (Genesis 3:21 Amplified).

God put the animal skin around Adam and Eve and covered them with the bloody garment that had been stripped off of an animal. This was the beginning of The Blood Covenant in Scripture. God made a Blood Covenant with a man named Abraham. We are partakers, even to this day, of that Blood Covenant through Jesus Christ.

The Blood Covenant

The Blood Covenant is beautifully seen in The Marriage Covenant. In biblical times, when a man and a woman, in the purest sense of a marriage, entered into the marriage chamber, God had planned that one man be with one woman for life. This meant that they had not entered into any sexual relationship with any other person except that one man or one woman. It was one man and one woman in holy matrimony, for life.

This is the beauty of The Blood Covenant. When it came time for the man to consummate the marriage, he would go into the bedroom with his virgin. At some point, the virgin would bleed. The blood shed created a blood covenant. After the marriage was consummated, the husband would take the sheets off of that sacred bed of matrimony, and he would run to the window to show the bloody sheet to the waiting wedding party outside. He was signifying that she was pure and that the marriage had been consummated. The Blood Covenant has been performed and **"what God has joined together, let no man or woman put asunder!"** This was the blood covenant of marriage.

The Salt Covenant

There is a second covenant. The Blood Covenant speaks of "redemption," but The Salt Covenant speaks of **"responsibility."** The Scripture says, "Season all your grain offerings with salt. Do not leave the salt of the covenant of your God out of your grain offerings; add salt to all your offerings" (Leviticus 2:13).

That salt was discussed in Jesus' writings, sermons, and teachings. In Mark 9, Jesus said, "For everyone shall be salted with fire. Salt is good; but if salt has lost its saltiness, how will you restore the saltiness to it? Have salt within yourselves, and be at peace and live in harmony with one another" (v 49-50 Amplified). This was the custom in the Middle East. The salt speaks of something very powerful. Salt was what made it pure and what made it clean.

We have a lot of people who offer God the sacrifice of praise, but there's no personal purity and holiness in their lives. But a song of praise or worship from a pure and clean vessel is a sweet aroma of sound in the Father's ears. Salt your praise with the sacrifice of a pure life. Jesus is the Bread of Life come down. Be willing to offer the salt sacrifice of a personal, holy life before God! It's a powerful thing.

Do you know why you're losing your spiritual power? You're not bringing any salt to your Christianity. If all you do is have grace, if you just think "I'm covered; I have fire insurance, so at least I'm not going to Hell," you are going to feel defeated a lot! But if you want some victory, you need some personal standards and convictions in line with God's Word.

We're not **"hearers of the Word only, we are doers of the Word!"** I can remember when I was a boy and would visit my granddaddy in North Carolina. Sometimes we would get in his pickup truck and drive out into the the cow pasture with a load of salt. We'd throw that salt off the truck and the cows would come running. You know what they did? They licked that salt like it was honey because there's something in creatures that crave salt.

Did you know your human body will die if you don't have salt? You were created with a need for salt. Well, the church is the Body of Christ, and I believe there's something missing today in modern Christianity. There is a craving going on among the real people of God that says, "Lord, I want to be separate and different for You!" Salt! Oh, Lord, we need a generation of salty Christians!

Covenant of Salt for Marriage

The Covenant of Salt for marriage is a Hebrew tradition. When a man and a woman wanted to enter into holy matrimony in ancient biblical days, she would bring her bag and pouch of salt. Understand, wages were paid through salt. The word "sal" from which we get "salary" is a Spanish word. "Sal" is a root for the word "salary." Salt was precious.

If a man and a woman wanted to make a commitment to each other, she would take a pinch of his salt and place it in her pouch. Then he would take a pinch of her salt and place it in his pouch. The man would then begin to declare the vows of the covenant that he was entering while he was shaking his bag of salt and saying these words:

"I promise to love you – I promise to be faithful to you – I promise to be true – I make this commitment till death do we part – I'll never leave you – I'll never forsake this covenant – this is a Covenant of Salt."

It meant this: If you can separate the salt grains that she put in there from mine, then and only then can this agreement be annulled.

The bride would then shake her bag and make her vows of commitment to her husband. They would promise to love each other and to always be faithful to each other. They would promise to always cherish and love each other and vow that nothing would ever separate them. They would proclaim to each other that when the grains of salt in their bags could be separated in the same manner they were put in…then, and ONLY then, could they ever be separated.

This "Covenant of Salt" was a powerful and sacred moment. God honors covenants today the way He did thousands of years ago.

Encounter

What about you? What kind of covenant are you willing to make, even as you read this book? Realize that keeping your covenant with God is critical to keeping your covenant in marriage. Your faithfulness to one another is reflective of your faithfulness to God.

Engage

Declare today, right where you are, the covenant you are wanting to declare:

Real Solutions

I need advice with my recently retired husband—now he wants to be with me 24/7! He's driving me crazy! What should I do?

Put him to work with a lengthy list of everything you ever wanted to get done! He'll avoid you like the plague. If that doesn't work, take him shopping with you at the mall . . . and just be yourself.

What does he enjoy doing without you? Feed that. Make purchases that encourage his hobbies; help him explore those options. Men tend to find their identity in what they do, and when what they do is no longer an option, the only other identity he has is his relationship with you.

Take inventory of interests and feed those desires with things to do.

CHAPTER 10

Seasoned with Salt--The Spice of Marriage

"

"You don't love someone because they're perfect;
you love them in spite of the fact that
they're not." —Jodi Picoult

"

Have you ever tasted food and something was missing? Maybe it was green beans, but something just didn't taste right? Maybe it was mashed potatoes or a salad, or really it could be just about anything, because nine times out of ten, the missing ingredient is salt. That little, tiny ingredient called salt makes a huge difference in a meal. Colossians 4:6 holds the key to a huge difference in your marriage and your walk with God: "Let your conversation be always full of grace, seasoned with salt, so that you may know how to answer everyone."

Let your words always be with grace, seasoned– there it is, the missing ingredient – "seasoned with salt," that you may know how to talk to one another. One of the greatest impediments of your spiritual growth and your marriage is that little ingredient--salt. It's your words. It's what you are saying. It's what's coming out of your mouth on a daily basis.

For me as a pastor and a man, it's the fact that I can preach and I can sing and yet, if my tongue is not bridled, it can do great harm to not only others but to myself as well. Jesus and the writers of the New Testament said we cannot praise God and then turn around and curse men with the same tongue. We cannot glorify Jesus one moment and criticize someone the next. There's the breakdown. This is where people lose the peace and the joy and the victory. We're supposed to have salt in our speech.

What does salt do? Salt preserves; it stops items from rotting. Salt preserves relationships; it preserves joy. When you have salt you're reserved in what you say, knowing those words have the power of life and death. When your speech is seasoned with salt, you're in control and careful and deliberate about what you say. It preserves the blessings you receive. It retains the joy and the peace. It preserves families; it preserves marriages; it preserves relationships.

Salt heals wounds. The old remedy used by many, including doctors, before there were antibiotics, was to pour salt on a wound because they recognized there's healing in salt. God said our speech is to be seasoned with salt. Our words are to heal not to wound, to heal not to accuse, to heal not to attack. This is especially true in your marriage and in parenting.

You can be saved, you can be on your way to Heaven, and you can even be filled with the Holy Spirit, and yet you can have a miserable life, all because you do not have your speech salted and directed by the Holy Spirit. Paul challenged the Colossians that their speech would be full of grace and favor. Grace when somebody messes up or somebody fails. Grace when someone doesn't live up to your expectations. Grace in your marriage when everything in you wants to criticize, nag, or vent. Your speech is to be seasoned with salt -– that you may know how to answer one another. When you speak, do you give people a second chance? When you hear somebody mess up, do you give them a second chance? Our words are to be seasoned with grace and favor. Do you look for the good?

The Measure of a Person

One of the greatest life lessons that you can learn is this: You can tell more about a person by what he says about others than by what others say about him. If you hear someone trashing other people all the time, you can mark it down that this person is a very judgmental, condemning person, and if they are talking about others who aren't present, they will talk about you the same way when you aren't there. The test for yourself is a simple one; it doesn't matter what other people say about you, it's what you say about others that really shows who you are.

Isaiah saw the Lord high and lifted up, and the first thing he said when he got in the holy presence of God was, "O, my God, what have I been saying?" We talk about everybody and everything as though our words have no consequences, and we forget that we are seen by God. Our negative words about others can condemn us and stop the joy from flowing into our lives.

We've forgotten that the doorway to happiness, life, peace, joy and healthy relationships is our mouth. In Matthew 12:36-37 Jesus said, "But I tell you, that men will have to give an account on the day of judgment for every careless word they have spoken. For by your words you will be acquitted, and by your words you will be condemned."

We, who are under no condemnation from God, with our own words can condemn ourselves, and we can speak life or death into our marriages. I can negate all the study, all the fasting, and all the prayer if my speech condemns me. I can negate them all when I talk too much. By our speech and our conversation we can invoke condemnation that will hang over our lives and rob us of joy and even years of our lives.

There is a passage in Hebrews Chapter four that says it like this:

Therefore, since we have a great high priest who has gone through the heavens, Jesus the Son of God, let us hold firmly to the faith we profess (v 14).

One translation says, "Jesus is the High Priest of our confession." What comes out of our mouth is a gift to the High Priest, Jesus. He then is responsible to present what comes out of our mouth to the Father, and the Father then is to bless or multiply and send back into our life what we offer as a gift from our mouth to our High Priest, for you and your marriage, and for your household.

Jesus, the high priest, takes our words of faith or unbelief--joy or anger. He takes our words of intercession or accusation and He presents them to the Father, every day of our life. Then the Father, in return, takes whatever you bring from your mouth and puts it back into your life. This explains why there are so many miserable, joyless Christians who are going to Heaven but not enjoying the journey and not enjoying their marriage, their family, their friends, and the many blessings God has given---because they are reaping what they speak.

We get back whatever we offer up with our mouths. Say this out loud right where you are: *"I get back whatever I offer up with my words, with my mouth."* Say this. *"Every day of my life, I get back from God what I offer up with my mouth."* When I talk to you in conversation, God is hearing it, and when I talk about you in conversation, God is hearing it. Those things that I'm saying are going to come back to me, in one way or another. Many Christians are doing everything right, living real holy lives, but their tongues are unbridled and words are like nitroglycerin. They can blow up a bridge or heal a man's heart. Many marriages are comprised of two people doing many good things, but their unbridled tongue is attracting condemnation instead of life and joy.

By your words you will be justified, by your words you will be condemned, and the devil's job is to get us so upset with somebody – a husband, a wife, a relative, a neighbor, a coworker – that you just talk about it and talk about it and talk about it and talk about it and it never goes away and you talk about it.

James 3 says it like this:

My brethren, let not many of you become teachers, knowing that we shall receive a stricter judgment. For we all stumble in many things. If anyone does not stumble in word, he is a perfect man, able also to bridle the whole body. Indeed, we put bits in horses' mouths that they may obey us, and we turn their whole body. Look also at ships: although they are so large and are driven by fierce winds, they are turned by a very small rudder wherever the pilot desires. Even so the tongue is a little member and boasts great things.

See how great a forest a little fire kindles! And the tongue is a fire, a world of iniquity. The tongue is so set among our members that it defiles the whole body, and sets on fire the course of nature; and it is set on fire by Hell. For every kind of beast and bird, of reptile and creature of the sea, is tamed and has been tamed by mankind. But no man can tame the tongue. It is an unruly evil, full of deadly poison. With it we bless our God and Father, and with it we curse men, who have been made in the similitude of God. Out of the same mouth proceed blessing and cursing. My brethren, these things ought not to be so. Does a spring send forth fresh water and bitter from the same opening? Can a fig tree, my brethren, bear olives, or a grapevine, bear figs? Thus no spring yields both salt water and fresh (v 3-12 NKJV).

I find it so easy to say something that I later regret, especially with my wife or one of my kids. Ignorance yearns to speak. Silence is a hard thing to argue with. We wonder where the victory is in our lives only to find we spoke it away. What if we, instead of hearing accusations and speaking accusations, would do what Jesus said and bless our enemies and pray for those who do us wrong (especially when it's a family member). We are to be peacemakers, we are to be healers, we are to be preservers, but too often we grieve the Holy Spirit with our words.

Has it ever crossed your mind or entered your heart that maybe instead of accusing you should be interceding? Maybe we need the fire from Heaven to touch our big mouth and season our speech with salt. What would happen if every one of us became seekers of a flaming tongue that had been purged? I mean, what would happen if we got desperate and became embarrassed because of the words that we have said? Refuse to accuse. This is not a game. The words that proceed from our mouths are life or death spiritually.

What's coming out of our mouths is victory or defeat. It's peace and joy or misery.

There's not a person reading this book that doesn't have a family situation or a family member that just rubs everybody wrong. What if we refuse to accuse and said, "I will not be an accuser. I will be an intercessor, and I'll season my words with salt." I want the Holy Spirit to give us fiery tongues, speech seasoned with salt.

What's the atmosphere of your marriage, your home, your life, your friends, and your co-workers? Maybe God wants you to be the salt in the conversation, so that when it starts going in the wrong direction, you change it and go a different route.

There is so much good news that you can take from this chapter because the one that decides what flows from your mouth is you. The one who makes the decision to speak life or death from this point on is you. How many times have you chosen to speak death rather than life in your marriage? If you are like most marriages, that number is a high number, but that can all change today with a simple decision.

Charles Spurgeon wrote these powerful words many, many years ago, and they are as true today as they were then:

The reputations of the Lord's people should be very precious in our sight, and we should count it shame to help the devil dishonor the Church and the name of the Lord. One of these dark days we may ourselves need forbearance and silence from our brethren; let us render it cheerfully to those who require it now. **Be this our family rule, and our personal bond---Speak evil of no man.**

—Charles Spurgeon, Morning and Evening November 29

How much stronger would your home be if this were your family rule and your personal bond?

Encounter

Salt preserves, salt heals, salt seasons. Which do you feel your marriage is most in need of right now? Preserving, healing or seasoning? Journal below about how the Lord spoke to you in this chapter:

....

....

....

....

....

....

Engage

Take a moment right now and ask God to restore your salt. Ask Him to bring back the joy of your salvation, the thrill of your young romance. Ask Him to add grace and kindness to your words. Ask Him for wisdom to know when silence is the best response.

....

....

....

....

....

....

....

My husband snores terribly. It's so bad that we sometimes sleep in separate rooms. Isn't this unhealthy for marriage? Help!!

Yes it is, and it's so unnecessary. There are so many devices and even medical interventions that can put an end to this tomorrow. Make an appointment with a doctor, or better yet, stay up after midnight and channel surf for the infomercials. I guarantee you; you will find three snoring devices within an hour. You may find it to be the best investment in your marriage you have ever made!

CHAPTER 11

The Cave of Couples

> ❝
> "To be fully seen by somebody, and be loved anyhow–this is a human offering that can border on miraculous."—Elizabeth Gilbert
> ❞

I saw something recently that I thought was pretty interesting. In the Spanish language, unlike English, nouns are designated masculine or feminine. One day in a university class a student thought it would be funny to ask, "What gender is a computer?" The professor thought for a moment and then, instead of answering the question directly, she split the class up into two groups; female students in one group and male students in the other and told the groups to decide which gender a computer was.

The men in the class got together and decided that computers are feminine. They gave the following four reasons:

1. No one but their creator understands their internal logic.

2. The native language they use to communicate with other computers is incomprehensible to everyone else.

3. Even the smallest mistakes are stored in long-term memory for later retrieval.

4. As soon as you make a commitment to one, you find yourself spending half your paycheck for accessories.

After having some fun with that, the ladies stepped up and took their shot at it. The teacher asked the women, and they said the computer is definitely masculine. They gave the following reasons:

1. Before you can get them to do anything, you have to turn them on.

2. They have a lot of data but still can't think for themselves.

3. They're supposed to help you solve problems, but half of the time they ARE the problem.

4. As soon as you commit to one, you realize if you had waited a little longer you could have gotten a better model.

While these conclusions are certainly less than scientific, they do represent the stereotypical lenses through which the two genders see the opposite gender. Truth is, men and women are different, and that was God's plan from the beginning. It certainly verifies that the Creator of the universe, and all creation, has a sense of humor.

There is a remarkable little passage of scripture that I pray God burns into your heart like He has in mine while I was preparing this chapter. It speaks of a cave purchased by Abraham.

Then Abraham stood up and bowed himself to the people of the land, the sons of Heth. And he spoke with them, saying, "If it is your wish that I bury my dead out of my sight, hear me, and meet with Ephron the son of Zohar for me, that he may give me the cave of Machpelah which he has, which is at the end of his field. Let him give it to me at the full price, as property for a burial place among you" (Genesis 23:7-9 NKJV).

The Bible says that there was a cave of Machpelah that Abraham bought. In verse 18 and 19, it goes on to say that Abraham buried Sarah, his wife, in the cave of the field of Machpelah. Then Genesis 49 talks about this same place. Scripture goes on to say that Abraham, Sarah, Isaac, Rebecca, and even Jacob were all buried in this same cave.

This is an interesting passage to me. "Machpelah" means "mach," or "cave." "Pelah" means "double." The cave of double or the cave of couples. That's what I want to talk about in this chapter: the cave of couples.

How do I keep my marriage together and make it all the way to the cave of couples? Abraham and Sarah ended their journey together in the cave of couples. Isaac and Rebekah were buried in the same cave because the parents set the example. The next generation, Isaac and Rebekah, felt like it didn't matter if they were not getting along perfectly, their parents modeled for them that they needed to stay together. They, too, were buried in the cave of couples. Then Jacob and Leah were buried in the cave of couples. How in the world do we get through this life, two totally different people, and end in the cave of couples?

Adam and Eve were the first couple that we read about in the Bible. God made them a couple and made them the example for all other couples who chose to follow God. He made man in His image, and then He took from Adam a rib and made woman. You may find yourself wondering sometimes, "Why a rib?" Here's the best explanation I have ever heard.

An angel came to Adam and said (paraphrased), "Adam, God wants to make you a beautiful companion. He's seen you lonely and He wants to bless you. She will be called 'woman.' She's going to be gorgeous. She's going to smell so sweet. When you come home from work, she's going to have your bedroom slippers all ready for you and she's going to be wearing your pajamas and she's going to usher you into your big chair and hand you your TV remote and the channel will already be set to ESPN. She's going to massage your shoulders. She's going to rub your feet just before she feeds you the gourmet meal prepared just for you, complete with dessert. And then after that, she is all yours for whatever you think you would care to do with her."

The man said, "Well, what is all that going to cost me?" And the angel said, "That's going to cost you your right arm and your left leg."

Adam thought for a moment, knowing that going without an arm and a leg would be quite a sacrifice. After some thought, the man asked, "Well...what can I get for just a rib?"

I will pause now to allow you time to recover from that lengthy and somewhat questionable answer to the age-old question: Why a rib?

The Bible said that God noticed that Adam was alone and there was nothing that had been created that was suitable for him. That's why when God brought Eve to Adam, he said, "She will be bone of your bone, flesh of your flesh." God was saying to Adam, " You are not an animal. I created you in my own image, different from anything else I have created. And from your rib, I have created 'woman' to be your companion." It's important to note that God didn't give him another man. God didn't give him three women. God made the first couple male and female.

To Build with Divine Help

The word "mate" is used to refer to the other "half" or the other "part." But when he describes the woman in Genesis, he calls her the "helpmeet," M-E-E-T. That is not a mispronunciation. That is a specific word for a specific reason. It's interesting that God called the wife the "helpmeet" not "helpmate." The Hebrew word is 'nezer.' It's the word from which we get "Ebenezer." The word "Ebenezer" is fairly common in the south. If you live in the south, somewhere in your town there's probably a church called Ebenezer Baptist Church.

That name comes from the story of Israel fighting the Philistines. The Philistines were about to slaughter them, but God started throwing hailstones from Heaven, and so the battle turned, and His people were delivered. The Bible says that the Israelites built a memorial to God and called it Ebenezer. "Eber," which means "to build," and "nezer" which means "divine help." **To build with divine help.** In other words, the only way they made it through the battle was with divine help. When God speaks of the wife, He says she is your "divine help," your Ebenezer. That's why the Bible says, "Whoever finds a wife, or divine help, finds favor with the Lord."

God looked at man and He said the number one need of man is not the need to breed; his number one need is divine help. If he's going to fulfill the call, purpose, and plan of God for his life, He is going to need divine help. Eve was God's spiritual help for Adam in a divine package. She was the divine help Adam needed, and your wife is the divine help that you're going to need every step of your life on the journey into God's plan for you and your family.

Adam had a relationship with God before he had Eve. He would walk with God an hour in the cool of the day through the garden. But God looked at him and said, "You know, it's good that I visit with you one hour a day, but you need somebody 23 other hours of the day, so I'm going to give you divine help in a human package. I'm going to give you a wife and she's going to be your helpmeet. She's going to be your nezer. I'm going to call it your 'easer.' And as long as you have her, you're going to have my divine help through her. I will bless you because of her in your life. You have obtained favor from the Lord."

YOUR Divine Help

You're going to win or lose your battles depending on whether you have divine help in your corner. You need divine help praying for you when you go to your job. You need some divine help aiding you as you raise those children. You need divine help building that career and that business. Without her, the divine help that you need will not be there.

You better cherish her. You better appreciate her. You better love her because she is your 'easer.' She'll ease your burdens and she will be your divine assistance.

Women are multipliers. Women are incubators. Women increase anything you give them, and if a man gives a woman a seed, she'll incubate it, she'll multiply it, she'll increase it, and nine months later, she'll give him back a baby. If you give a woman your bachelor pad after you get married, she'll incubate it, multiply it, and increase it. You'll get furniture, you'll get curtains; you'll get more than just a house, you'll get a home. It won't look like a battle zone from the battle of Armageddon. It will look like something that divine help got ahold of; she'll multiply it and give it back to you in a much better condition.

It never ceases to amaze me how many women fight depression because their husbands are successful and they build huge corporations, leaving no time for family. In that kind of success for the man, the woman can be made almost to feel unimportant and unnecessary. And this is just as true if the roles are reversed. I'll speak about my own life. Whatever little success I've had, people do not realize the impact my wife has had on it. The truth is, without my wife's divine help, this ministry wouldn't be here. I wouldn't be writing this book.

I say to wives today, you are important. You matter. You can make a difference because you are the divine help. You're the difference for whether your husband wins or loses. Your husband needs divine help in a human package, and you are that package.

Psalm 127 says, *"Unless the Lord builds the house, its builders labor in vain."* God's way is to give you divine help in the form of that precious spouse of yours. You had better treat her right because she's your anointing. She's your favor. How you treat her will determine how God listens to your prayers. She's your divine help, and when you begin thinking that you're really something and you begin ignoring her, belittling her, and acting as though you've done it all yourself, you need to stop right in your tracks and remember that she is your divine help sent by God. When the Lord builds the house, we're striving together, we're praying together, we're dreaming together, we're doing the Lord's will together, we're raising our kids together, we're building a house together, and we're doing life together.

Cave of Couples

Abraham's wife Sarah died at age 127, and Abraham was surprised because he had always thought he would go first since he was ten years older. The Bible said he panicked a bit and said, "*I have got to have a burial place for my precious wife*" and bought the cave of double, the cave of couples, Machpelah.

In Judaism, the cave of Machpelah is the second most holy site in Israel. It's where Abraham and Sarah, Isaac and Rebekah, and Jacob and Leah are all buried. Tourists go there and teach their children its meaning; there are ceremonies and family dedications; it is the ultimate place that you can reach in a couple's relationship. We need to realize that every day we are setting the example for our children. We must make sure we set the example that says, "till death do we part."

It's not a one-man show. I don't want a man-cave. I want a couple's cave. I don't understand men who leave their wives all the time to hang out with their buddies. It's okay to get with the guys and have fun every once in awhile, but my God, when you're doing life, you're not to spend all your time in a man-cave, you were put together by God to live in a couple-cave. You should do everything together as much as you can. And you should never have any friend that matters more to you than your wife or your husband does.

Fight for What's Left

You will remember that "pelah" means "double." If you stay together, and if you make it to the cave of couples, you get double. You get double the strength. You get double the protection over your children and your grandchildren. You get double the favor of God. You get double the prosperity. The enemy cannot destroy the home that says, "We're going to the cave of couples, and divorce isn't going to get our marriage, and it's not going to get our children's marriage and our children's children marriage. By the grace of God, we will not quit."

I have a preacher friend who told me that he went to a funeral of a pastor's son. His 16-year-old son was killed tragically in a car wreck, and the mother, the pastor, and the siblings, were sitting on the front row devastated, as the 16-year-old body of their brother and their son was laying in that coffin. I asked my friend, "What did you preach on? What do you say to a family like that that's been devastated?" He told me that he preached on Rizpah. Rizpah in the Old Testament had five sons, and the Gibeonites invaded and hung all five of her sons. While they were hanging from the tree, she took a bat and beat away the wild animals and kept the buzzards off of her children, and she pitched a tent and sat on a rock for three months and wouldn't let the animals devour the bodies of her boys even though they were dead. My preacher friend said, "I preached on the topic, 'Fight for what's left.'"

I don't care how bad the enemy has devastated you. I don't care if there's been infidelity. Maybe you've been shocked, you've been hurt, you've been broken. I'm telling you that God can heal, God can restore, God can fix, and God can bring back. Fight for what's left. That's why you're reading this book. The enemy may have attacked your family, but it's not perfect families that make it to the cave of couples. It's families that have been through hell, but they have the grace of God and have declared, "We'll fight for what's left!" God can give you the grace to recover it all. He can restore what the enemy tried to take from you, the same way He has done for countless others.

God says that if you'll give him your family, along with all the lies, the lust, and the losers, He can touch it with His grace and can make winners out of that house. He can bless and anoint that house. You don't have to give up and you don't have to quit. It's not perfect and flawless people in the cave of couples. It's people who refused to give in or take the easy way out. It is people who surrendered the right to themselves and exchanged that right for a promise and a cave.

Research shows that, statistically, the happiest couples are those who have been married 30 to 35 years. It typically takes the first 9 to 17 years for people to die to self. That's why the highest percentage of divorces occur during the first 9 years of marriage. We need to understand that some days are good and some days are tough, You need to declare to your spouse, "You're going to be buried by me, and I'm going to be buried by you." We're going to the cave of couples and divorce simply cannot be an option.

We are all deeply flawed. I know of nothing on earth that exposes and displays selfishness the way marriage can. Marriage is brutal on selfishness. We are all imperfect people, and that has been the case for man throughout history. We all mess up and we all make mistakes. We all say cruel things, and we all do stupid things. For me, I can build churches and I can preach and I can win souls, but what would it all be worth if at the end of life my wife has lost respect for me because I didn't have integrity, because I didn't have character, or because I didn't do it right? I have to treat her like she's my divine help.

The Lord spoke to me when I was studying for this chapter, and He said, "How would you treat her if she was your anointing? How would you treat her if she was your revelation of the Bible? How would you treat her if she was the key to you being able to effectively touch the congregations that you minister to? How would you treat her all week long?" That ripped my heart out because I don't want to get to the end of my life and my wife not even want to be in the cave of couples with me. I want her to respect me and love me. I want my children and my grandchildren to love me and honor me.

Going Deeper

I'm happy for you young couples because right now you're in love and you can't keep your hands off each other. I mean, I love it when I see newlyweds. I don't want to lose that with Cherise. But the only way you're going to hold it together is to keep going deeper and deeper into Jesus. We have something greater that will hold us together. Every time life happens, we're going to go deeper into Him. We don't let trials, troubles, issues and problems stop us. We go deeper into Him. He's the answer. I don't care what's hanging on you, when you get in Him, you can handle it.

Husbands and wives in the 21st century need to declare to each other, "You and I are going to end of our journey together. I love you. You're my divine help and you are the 'easer' of my life. We lived together and we will be buried together. We said 'Till death do we part' and nothing's going to ever change that. Don't you ever question that. Don't you ever worry about that. We're not a perfect couple, and the Lord knows we have our flaws, but we also have God's grace."

Remember the vows you made to each other. Determine to walk this road together all the way to the cave of couples. No quitting, no giving up. Go deeper into Jesus no matter what life brings.

Encounter

I believe your spouse is a gift from God to you. Do you believe that? Do you believe your mate is your divine help? Have you treated them like they are a gift from God? Journal below about what you believe to be true about your spouse and how you have treated your spouse and interacted together.

....

....

....

....

....

....

Engage

Acknowledge to God that you believe your spouse has a purpose in His Kingdom and a purpose in your life. After you've prayed, take a moment and write down any ways that come to your mind about what you need to do differently in your interactions and view of your spouse.

....

....

....

....

....

....

Real Solutions

We have two small children. How can I maintain the balance between time for my marriage and having 2 kids that constantly demand my attention?

1. *Bedtime as an early and regular routine.*

2. *Utilize local family, and if you don't have local family that can help, then*

3. *You need to be in a small group with couples in your life-stage and find ways to share the load. Bottom line; make time where you can have kid-free evenings or even days.*

4. *Try to stake out one night a week as a date night and guard it every week. A good baby sitter may be the best investment you can make in your marriage in this stage of parenting.*

Section

04

Marriage in the 21st Century

CHAPTER 12

Cause and Effect--The Marriage Dance

> **"**
> Let the wife make the husband glad to come home, and let him make her sorry to see him leave.
> —Martin Luther
> **"**

Many Americans are forgoing marriage altogether. At the same time, the share of children born outside of marriage now stands at 41%, up from just 5% in 1960. One of the largest shifts in family structure is this: 34% of children today are living with an unmarried parent—up from just 9% in 1960, and 19% in 1980. And thousands of children are not living with either parent. In most of these cases, they are living with a grandparent—a phenomenon that has become much more prevalent since the recent economic recession.

God Has a Plan--A Good Plan

Is it any wonder that Jesus spoke so clearly about marriage and placed such an emphasis on strengthening marriages and giving guidelines for godly living and the importance of love and obedience in all things? Ever since the Garden of Eden, Satan has fought against the marriage covenant.

The enemy is bringing divorce, drugs, alcoholism, greed, and lust to bear on our families and marriages to destroy them. That is why we must have godly fathers who will be the priest, the prophet, and the king of the homes and stand up and cover their families and marriages in the blood of Jesus. We need men who will take the time to build their homes on the rock of Christ Jesus and who will be able to weather the storms of life successfully. These men will have godly offspring.

God's plan is marriage, and He said the marriage bed should be undefiled. We need to

---

be willing to tell our young people that there is an appropriate time for sex, and that time is when you are married. The scripture says that you are committing sin if you enter into sexual activity outside of marriage.

The Enemy Wants to Destroy Your Home

Scripture reveals that God's plan is marriage between one man and one woman. Genesis is the book of Beginnings, and Satan started in the very beginning hitting marriage with sin. As soon as he saw God's plan he began to attack: In Genesis 3, it's man vs. woman. In Genesis 4, we see polygamy. In Genesis 9, it's pornography (pornography is lustful looking). Then in Genesis 16, it's adultery. In Genesis 19, it's homosexuality. In Genesis 34, it's fornication. In Genesis 38, it's incest and prostitution, and in Genesis 39, it's seduction. From homosexuality to pornography to polygamy--you name it, Satan did everything he could to destroy marriage, and he started in the book of Genesis.

Millions of men father children and just walk away. Did you know that the average dad in America spends two minutes a day in meaningful conversation with his children? Two minutes a day! Former Secretary of Education and member of the National Security Advisory Counsel Bill Bennett stated that over the last two decades there has been a 550% increase in violent crimes, 400% increase in illegitimate births, 2000% increase in teen pregnancy, and a 300% increase in teen suicide. If you take a close look at who is in American jails, 70% of the inmates come from fatherless homes, and 79% of the people who are addicted to drugs are addicted because a void was created due to a fatherless home.

Communication is the Key

Communication is the key. Put down the paper, turn off the TV, and begin to talk. Get on the same page about your week. Talk about your day, make plans, and begin to include each other in the conversations of life.

The enemy is bringing many evils against the home: divorce, drugs, drunkenness, homosexuality, greed, adultery, and pornography on the internet. He is using these perversions to destroy marriages and homes. We are living in a confused society. Boys are carrying purses. Girls are carrying footballs. You don't know if it's a Mr. or a Mrs. There is enough in the world to create confusion and chaos. But there is a better way. We need to understand that God doesn't save us **in** our sins, He saves us **from** our sins when we really get saved. One simple decision can change everything, be that following

Christ for the first time, rededicating your life to walk in His ways, or simply deciding that from this day forward, you are going to set your focus on Christ and begin to walk in His ways. CHANGE is possible. As for you and your family… Only you can complete that sentence. Choose your words wisely.

Encounter

"I don't know and I don't care" cannot be the mantra of your marriage. Nor do I think it is, or you wouldn't be reading this book. But perhaps you've had that attitude in the past. Ask God to show you areas of apathy in your life specifically related to your marriage.

Engage

Think of at least one way you can take a more proactive role in making your marriage better. Make sure this is something you can do and not something that depends on the actions of your spouse.

Do you have any tips on how to add spark to our sex? Any recommendations?

First of all, to each his own . . . and everything consensual is legal inside the confines of marriage. That's all I am going to say in a PG rated book!

On a more serious note, while this may be difficult at first, every marriage expert I have ever heard or read says the number one key to an active, healthy, exciting sex-life is communication. Sometimes we just have to be honest with each other. The second most important thing is a willingness to try new things. The third thing is to realize that sex in marriage is not just about you. There may be things your partner wants to try that you really aren't into, but you go down that path because your spouse's experience matters to you. Like I said above, everything is legal . . . and the marriage bed is supposed to be everything Song of Solomon says and more.

CHAPTER 13

The Process of Marriage

> ❝
>
> To keep your marriage brimming with love in the loving cup, Whenever you're wrong, admit it; Whenever you're right, shut up. —Ogden Nash
>
> ❞

Why is it that the first thing we do after we get married is to try and make the other person just like us? I am about to share something with you about my wife, Cherise, but please don't share this with anyone else. I also ask that you extend grace and mercy to my dear wife. It used to really bug me, but here it is: Cherise puts sugar in her grits. I kid you not, You're probably asking yourself the same thing I asked, "What kind of person puts sugar in their grits?" To make matters worse, all my daughters started putting sugar in their grits. But you know, if you stay with it long enough, after a while you just start reaching for the sugar before they ever ask for it. You just evolve and realize that it's just not worth fighting over!

Five Steps to a Happier Marriage

1. You have to stop insisting that your partner be just like you. In a marriage, you have to continually ask yourself if the fight is really that important. God puts us together in hopes that we will balance each other out a little bit. One's too strict and the other's too loose. One's an early riser and one is a late riser. One likes McDonalds and the other likes Burger King. We stabilize one another, and that's a good thing. Give and take a little bit, and choose the hills you are willing to die on very wisely. There are no ceremonies for those losses.

When we were younger, when Cherise and I went on vacation, I would like to get up early and get my day started, but that wasn't a holiday to Cherise. She wanted to sleep in because she had to get up and go all the time with the children. What I had to learn to do in those situations was to not insist that she be just like me. We learned over the years to give each other some room. I'll get up with the sun and do my thing, and I'll come back a few hours later. I might go for a run, and when I get back she's just stirring. And that's OK. We have learned through the years to give each other that space and have our together time while allowing for the other person's alone time. You need to quit trying to make the other person be just like you! YOU don't even like yourself half the time.

2 You need to agree that separation is not going to be an option. I appreciate my mother-in-law Pat. She told Cherise when we first got married, "Now when you marry him, don't you come running back to my house unless he beats you or does something really bad to you. You're married, and separation is not an option!" Part of the strength of marriage is how you work out conflicts. A marriage never gets stronger if you don't go through conflicts and work them out. The more conflicts you go through and work out, the stronger your marriage gets! That's why I don't believe in separation. If you're married, you're married; stay together!

There are exceptions. If there is physical violence, addiction, or in cases of unrepentant adultery, separation can be a good thing for a season and until there can be counseling and changed behavior. But I'm NOT talking about two Christians who just aren't getting along. You need to realize you're married! There may be some issues you should have thought through ahead of time and before you said "I do," but if you separate, you're giving place to the devil, and not only are you taking the easy way out, you are operating outside the perfect will of your God.

In real marriages, both spouses need to say, "I know you won't leave" and allow fears and doubts to give way to trust and security. You need to say to each other, "Whatever happens, I'm not going anywhere, and you're not going anywhere."

3 Learn how to disagree, argue, and then move on. Healthy marriages leave the past in the past. If you're going to survive your relationship, you have to learn how to have an argument and then to move on, because conflict will come; it does in every relationship. But that's not to say that if we aren't careful, we can go past a breaking point, and when things break, they can be hard to put back together. We are commanded to forgive, but there's a difference between "forgiveness" and "trust." "Trust" when betrayed can break a heart, and that makes it difficult for a person to trust again. Trust must be earned, especially when trust has been violated previously or repeatedly. You may be thinking, "Well, they should be over it by now!" That depends on what you did! Trust cannot be demanded. Trust has to

be earned, and it takes time to get trust back.

I've been pastoring for almost thirty years, and believe me when I say that I have just about seen it all. One of the big problems that I see that is destroying marriages more than anything is internet pornography, especially for men. Through the years, when I've had to personally get involved, it seems that once the wife caught the man looking at pornography, there was a "trust" in that marriage that was broken, sometimes fatally.

The real danger in pornography, as it relates to the marriage relationship, is in the desensitization that occurs toward a real, in-person, spouse. An article in The Sun newspaper entitled "Porn Addiction Turning Men Into Hopeless Lovers" talked about the effects of porn on the male brain and speaks to the issues pornography addiction can have on the physical relationship of the couple:

Guys go in expecting it to all be easy and they don't know what to do, (because that is how it is in pornography). Dr. Angela Gregory, a sex therapist at Nottingham University Hospital, added: "Men are becoming both physically and psychologically desensitized to normal sexual stimulation and arousal with a sexual partner. Real romance can sometimes fail to satisfy the porn-primed appetites of smut addicts." Experts warn that all porn junkies pay a heavy price for their addiction. Says Gregory, "They may also become hooked on extreme porn depicting acts that few women would be willing to endure, leaving them bored by the standard sex offered with real life partners."

The problem is compounded by the omnipresence of online pornography, which means extreme content can be found free of charge in little more than a few clicks. Anothr ex and relationship columnist, Dr. Pam Spurr, said researchers have noticed a "huge increase in younger men who use porn regularly and can't (have normal sex) when with a (live) partner." She wrote: "They've become so used to masturbating to porn that they find it hard to relate to a partner. Or because they're used to the excitement of porn films they don't get aroused by 'ordinary' sex. The fantasy sex in porn is what they expect now. They need all that fakery – the physically enhanced bodies, the fantasy scenarios, the XXX-rated kinky things some porn stars do."

This excerpt is from a secular publication, and even in a secular publication, they acknowledge the dangers of pornography on relationships. As a pastor, I see this all of the time, and I see the confusion and the desperation of men who love the Lord but cannot seem to help themselves in moments of weakness. Simply stated, there are some things you can have (such as alcohol, drugs, and pornography), but in far too many cases, at some point, it has you.

Many men are able to compartmentalize the time they spend looking at pornography and completely believe it has nothing to do with their love for their spouse, their love for their family, or even their walk with Christ. In reality, they are living a lie. Many times the men say to me, "It's been three months and she still won't forgive me." These men genuinely feel like this was somehow unfair. They fail to grasp the magnitude of the infidelity of their actions. This is the desensitization that the article above spoke of. They fail to realize that trust takes time, and rebuilding trust can take even longer, and rebuilding trust cannot even begin without addressing the core issue, which is pornography.

Nearly all women severely react to infidelity, and most women do not see infidelity on the internet as being any different than infidelity in person. Many men wrongly see it as two very different things. Sometimes, when we're watching a show, the main character will kill somebody and they're going to give him the electric chair, and Cherise will say, "They shouldn't do that; he's cute." But if he cheated on his wife and committed petty theft, she will yell from the couch, "They should fry him!" Her grace and mercy meter goes into hibernation!

If you've been on the receiving end of a violation in your marriage, it doesn't need to sabotage your marriage for the rest of your life. As the offended one, you hold the power of death or life over that marriage, and you have every right to be upset and untrusting. I get that. But I am here to tell you that there is another way. Forgiveness is possible, and God can still perform a miracle in your marriage. Remember that whatever decision you make in that hour will have a lasting effect and impact on the entire family, yourself included, for the rest of your life.

When you refuse to forgive --when you keep the wall up –you are not doing yourself any good, and refusing to forgive is as useless as standing in a hurricane with an umbrella. At some point, you have to value yourself, especially if you've been hurt, and choose grace and mercy. Sometimes we have to reach out beyond justice to a place called mercy or else risk never loving again.

4 Keep your comments about your spouse's family to yourself. When you join yourself together with that person, you join yourself together with their family (to a degree). I know the Bible says, "Let a man leave his mother and father, and cleave unto her husband, or his wife." You need to try to make things work. You need to try to get along with each other's families. But there are going to be conflicts, and it's wise to keep your comments to yourself! You need to learn that one. When you go to family events, sometimes you just need to bite

your tongue. Never allow intrusions from anybody to drive a wedge between you and your spouse.

At some point you have to have some boundaries and say, "We love you. We want to be a part of this family. Let's agree on the things we can agree on, and let's avoid criticism. Let's just stay on neutral ground." Sometimes you just have to give it a little space until God works it out. We have been through it in our families. You just have to protect your marriage above all.

5 Did you know that the leading cause of divorce is finances? Years ago it was issues like infidelity or incompatibility. But in the hour we are in, finances is the leading cause and it has been for the last several years. So much of what you can and cannot do is linked to finances, credit scores and debt. We have watched for years as most people live paycheck to paycheck and have many months where the paycheck runs out before all the bills can be paid. Add to that the side jobs plus two working parents and the end result is incredible amounts of stress. Ladies, if you have a husband who doesn't make all that you want him to make, remember that your words can emasculate a man. You must choose your words wisely. Odds are, your role as a helpmeet will be needed more than ever. Keep talking and keep speaking life into each other.

If a man is going through a tough time bringing home enough money, it is a humiliating thing and he will lay awake for hours trying to figure out how to make it work. If he's doing his best and if he's working hard, you're blessed. You've got to stick together. That's what marriage is about. It's not about "attacking" one another. It's about doing the best you can. Even if you lose everything, you are still going to have each other.

Solution number one: in times like this, put the tithe up front. Make the tithe the very first thing you pay each month and see if God will not start coming through in amazing ways. It's a spiritual principle and one that could change your entire outlook.

Solution number two: Sit down and create a budget TOGETHER. Lay it all out there. This may be difficult for men to do, but they miss the valuable role the wife plays as their "divine help."

Solution number three: Avoid debt as much as possible. If you can't pay cash, don't buy it.

Solution number four: Ask for help. Go to your pastor and tell him you need help and see if your pastor(s) cannot match you with a godly couple who can walk with you and mentor you in this area.

There is hope in ALL things and in ALL seasons, and that goes for financial seasons of lack and plenty. Get on your knees and ask for guidance and wisdom.

I truly believe that the Lord has called me to tell each person reading this book, "In all seasons, be good to each other." Be friends with each other. Do you know how many people who are married are not even friends with each other? Did you get married to be apart? Be friends with one another! Keep your relationship tight. If you're drifting apart, work on it; do something. Grow beyond silent treatments and cold shoulders. Silent frustration tears apart inwardly. Keep it "tight." Don't let silent frustration simmer. Deal with it! Go to God – Forgive - Get up - Try again - Start over - Grab each other – Love each other – Fight - Make up. There's something about a marriage that if it goes through that process enough, out of it comes a strong relationship.

I want you to pray this prayer, and as you do, know that I have prayed this prayer over each and every person who will read this book.

Father, I pray for my marriage. I ask Your blessing over us in the name of the Father, the Son, and the Holy Ghost. I pray that You'll take what I've read, as only You can do, Holy Spirit, and bless our marriage and home. I pray for areas of conflict to be resolved. I pray hurts from the past we're holding onto will be released. I pray, God, if I am trying to make (spouse's name) into who I want (him/her) to be, I would see it, and begin to be more open to the fact that You put the two of us together to even out one another! Let me realize and celebrate our uniqueness. I praise You God for helping our marriage and blessing our home.

Encounter

What parts of this chapter spoke to your heart? Journal below about what you heard the Lord say to you as you read.

Engage

If God revealed to you any way that you have tried to force unnecessary change on your spouse, write it down. Then determine how you can begin to celebrate their uniqueness and the balance they bring to your relationship.

Real Solutions

My husband and I have been married 10 years. When we got married we were equally yoked. But since then I have grown so much in my faith and in the church and the Word. But my husband went the other way and never developed any interest in church or the things of the Lord. I want more love and more togetherness, but it seems the closer I get to the Lord, the further apart we get. What should I do?

This is a really common occurrence in the church in 2017, and has been for the last 15 years. Part of the problem is that we have so feminized the church experience that it has become unappealing for many men of today. Men are about adventure and risk, and our church services are more about singing, holding hands and emotion. But it's a real problem.

Second, men are drawn to Jesus in different ways than women. Look for that bridge. And if there are no bridges such as small group men's events, conferences, and other less threatening bridges, then you may need to look for another church.

And finally, never underestimate the power of a praying wife. I have seen many men in our altars while knowing this miracle came after years of prayer and intercession.

CHAPTER 14

Is Marriage Still a Good Idea?

> **"**
>
> Is marriage still a good idea? All married couples should learn the art of battle as they should learn the art of making love. Good battle is objective and honest - never vicious or cruel. Good battle is healthy and constructive, and brings to a marriage the principles of equal partnership.
>
> —Ann Landers
>
> **"**

Cherise and I were in California not too long ago, and we went in a restaurant and sat down to eat. Across the aisle was a couple who began to get in a knock down, smack down, fuss and fight argument. I'm talking veins bulging out of the forehead and neck. They were mad and throwing cuss words at each other to the point that it was getting awkward. Finally, after some intense fighting, they stomped out!

I don't know how it ended, but as they left, I said to Cherise, "I KNOW they're married." She replied, "How do you know they're married?" I answered, "Because it takes decades to fight that good. You don't learn how to fight that good just by dating; you have to be married to learn how to fight like that."

The title of this chapter is, "Is Marriage Still a Good Idea?" There are a lot of people who don't think it is any more, and that's sad. The movies you see today seem to have taken the position that marriage really isn't the best option, whereas living together is commonplace. You know the scenario: the married guys are out and about and they see an old friend they haven't seen in awhile. They ask him, "Are you single?" He says, "Yes," and they all give him high fives as if to say, "Lucky you!"

I recently came across an article on Facebook by Archit Tripathi entitled, "Hilarious Tweets About Married Life That Really Hit Home." The article says:

When the honeymoon is over, couples start getting real with each other. The key to a good marriage is compromise. Whether it's about who does what chores around the house or who's picking dinner, a healthy give-and-take ratio is what makes a long-lasting marriage possible. Of, course, venting on Twitter from time to time doesn't hurt either. Whether you've been married for ten years or ten days, every couple can relate to some of the tweets below:

Wife: It's like every man on earth has to share one brain!

Husband: Can't think of a good comeback because it's not my turn to use the brain.

Husband: My wife said I need to grow up! I was speechless. It's hard to respond with 45 gummy bears in your mouth.

Husband: My wife recently informed me that she wanted two kittens, but I am the man of the house...so we got two kittens.

(Out in public):

Husband: A kid is crying.

Wife: It's not one of ours.

(We fist-bump)

Wife to friends: *Sorry I was late. I had to find all the things that were in plain sight for my husband.*

Husband: *(pulls curtain back while wife is in the shower) Are we—STOP SCREAMING, it's just me. Are we out of Cheetos?*

Wife: *When my husband goes outside to investigate a strange noise, how long do I have to wait before unpausing the show we are watching?*

Husband: *When my wife falls asleep in a public place, I shake her a* *little and yell, "DON'T YOU DIE ON ME!" People always clap when she wakes up.*

And my personal favorite:

Husband: *Want me to make dinner?*

Wife: *Nah, it's ok honey, I know you're still tired from doing it back in 2003.*

Recently, the best selling author Elizabeth Gilbert, who wrote the book and eventual motion picture *Eat, Pray, Love,* wrote a new book called *Committed.* This is a book that experts are calling "a breakthrough book on relationships." The subtitle is "A Skeptic Makes Peace with Marriage." Gilbert has said for years and years that marriage is not necessary and that it's a broken institution. It just so happens that she met "Mr. Right" and married him. After some time in her marriage relationship she changed her position and declared, *"Marriage may not be a totally bad idea."*

In an interview recently, she said this, *"I feel like I'm starting a subversive movement by being pro-marriage."* That tells you something about the condition of our mentality in the 21ˢᵗ century when a woman says, *"I'm doing something that is really, really profound. I'm starting a subversive, or counter-culture movement, called being pro-marriage."*

That's how bad of a rap marriage has gotten in our society. But this is not a new thing, or even a product of modern day society. In Mark, Chapter 10, divorce had become very common, and the Pharisees came to Jesus wanting Him to make bigger loopholes so they could get divorces.

Then He arose from there and came to the region of Judea by the other side of the Jordan. And multitudes gathered to Him again, and as He was accustomed, He taught them again.

The Pharisees came and asked Him, "Is it lawful for a man to divorce his wife?" testing Him. And He answered and said to them, "What did Moses command you?"

They said, "Moses permitted a man to write a certificate of divorce, and to dismiss her."

And Jesus answered and said to them, "Because of the hardness of your heart he wrote you this precept. But from the beginning of the creation, God 'made them male and female.'

For this reason a man shall leave his father and mother and be joined to his wife, and the two shall become one flesh; so then they are no longer two, but one flesh. Therefore what God has joined together, let not man separate."

In the house His disciples also asked Him again about the same matter. So He said to them, "Whoever divorces his wife and marries another commits adultery against her. And if a woman divorces her husband and marries another, she commits adultery" (Mark 10:1-12 NKJV).

Not the answer they were looking for to be sure, and it's still not the answer people are looking for today when desiring the will of God for their marriage. Jesus was saying that marriage in its original meaning, and beginning, was meant to be between one man and one woman, for life, 'till death do we part.'

Far too many people today, and historically, believe it's not a big deal if you get divorced. They've adopted the mindset, "Try it, and if it doesn't work out, you can divorce and marry somebody else." But Jesus went on to teach that you don't get divorced because you're not getting along. Today, I want to reaffirm that marriage is not going to go away. Marriage is God's idea—it's here to stay—and it's the best way to do life, because God said it is!

I recently got a hold of a book called *Sexual Detours* by a man named Dr. Hines, and in it he gives these astonishing statistics:

- 70% of men will cheat on their wives.

- 60% of women will cheat on their husbands.

- 50% of every marriage will end in divorce – that's one out of two!

If you got up in the morning and turned on the news, and they said, "Warning, there are wild bears on the loose in northeast Georgia. Don't let your children go to the bus stop alone. If you do, there's a 50% chance they will be attacked by a wild bear." Would you just get up, put the backpack on your kid, and say, "Go to the bus stop, and if a bear chases you, run fast?" No, of course not! You wouldn't do that.

What if you saw on the news a warning that said, "Due to hazardous conditions, 50% of the cars on the highway will have a crash tomorrow morning." Would you at least take some precautions? Would you maybe NOT do your makeup in the rear view mirror as you drive? Or would you make sure not to text while you are driving? Or would you at least put your seatbelt on? I think you would! And yet, we hear statistics like this – one out of two marriages end in divorce, and we convince ourselves "It could never happen to me." And yet, it's happening to people in astonishing numbers.

Today I want to give you keys to **being the best mate you can be.** I want to give you the reasons that marriage is still a good idea. I want you to read and take this to heart, because if one out of two marriages end in divorce, and if 70% of men cheat and 60% of women cheat, we need to figure out why that is happening. Here are five keys to being a suitable mate. Spiritual compatibility matters--it always has, and it always will.

II Corinthians 6:14-16 says this:

Do not be yoked together with unbelievers. For what do righteousness and wickedness have in common? Or what fellowship can light have with darkness? What harmony is there between Christ and Belial? Or what does a believer have in common with an unbeliever? What agreement is there between the temple of God and idols? For we are the temple of the living God. As God has said: "I will live with them and walk among them, and I will be their God, and they will be my people."

Do not enter into a relationship that holds different values than you hold. If someone doesn't have the value system that you have, the moral system that you have, and the faith system that you have, do not get in a relationship with them.

Now, since you are already married, this passage needs to hit you in different ways depending on where you are in your relationship. **First,** if you married an unbeliever, you have your work cut out for you, but scripture holds out hope!

How do you know, wife, whether you will save your husband?

Or, how do you know, husband, whether you will save your wife? (I Corinthians 7:16)

There is hope and the knowledge that Jesus loves your spouse even more than you do.

Second, this issue of being unequally yoked really lies at the root of divorce in the church. You can both be Christians, saved by grace with your eternal security intact, and yet be at very different places in your walk with Christ. With most couples there is one that spends more time in the word, or serving, or in prayer than the other. One can literally be more spiritually mature than the other, and this 'gap' can result in division if you aren't careful. If you want your marriage to grow closer, then start growing closer to the Lord. It is literally a spiritual law that the closer you both draw to the Lord in the spiritual realm, the closer you are drawing to each other.

Are you praying daily? Do you read your Bible? Do you have a prayer place and a prayer time that you have set aside to spend time with the Lord? Are you praying together as a couple? Are you in God's house on a regular basis? Are you connecting with other believers in meaningful and authentic ways? These are the disciplines of the faith. I would love to tell you that all you need to do is go through your day and not worry about all these questions. But the fact is, relationships take work. Are you willing to do these simple daily tasks?

God knows how much a person's faith permeates their inner being when they're really saved. God knows that fully surrendering to Jesus Christ has massive implications. It changes the atmosphere in a home. It changes the way that you think when Jesus is truly Lord of your life. It changes the way you behave. It changes the way you love. It changes the way you handle your money. It changes what you do on the weekend. It changes who your friends are. It changes the places you feel comfortable going. It changes what you will do with your spare time.

When Jesus is truly Lord of your life, it has huge implications on your life. And when you're a fully devoted Christian, Jesus is not a "P.S." on the end of your week after you do what you want to do all week long. You don't just tip your hat at Him on Sunday through a little weak church service somewhere.

Jesus understands that when you're truly devoted to Him, it is a part of your core identity. It defines you. It's what happens in the deepest parts of you. Now imagine that kind of born again, spirit-filled relationship with Jesus Christ. When you take a person whose core identity is to please and honor Jesus Christ, and imagine them married to someone who doesn't give a rip about prayer, Jesus, His word, or His church, you are unequally yoked.

It's very difficult when a Christian is married to someone who cannot imagine why anyone would sit around reading something as old and archaic as the word of God. This is what many people experience because they break this first thing called "spiritual compatibility."

That's what God is trying to spare you from. I have seen it hundreds of times. Sometimes Cherise and I will have a conversation that sounds something like this; "Cherise, this morning when I was praying, or when I was reading the Bible, I feel like the Lord told me…". Sometimes she will tell me, "I read this scripture just the other day." That's powerful stuff!

I cannot imagine being married to someone and not being able to talk things over like that. I can't imagine raising our children and not being able to talk about spiritual matters and principles. You can both be Christian, but do you have the same intensity for Jesus Christ? Are you spiritually compatible?

Third: Communication. Some years back, I had to go take my license test again. It seemed kind of silly. I drive every day, so why do I have to study the book again? When it comes to communication and HOW to communicate, it pays off to go back to the Book and brush up on some very valuable spiritual principles. You may think, "We talk every day. We've been communicating for years now." Yet that's the problem when it comes to communication in marriage. You do it every day, but that doesn't mean you are doing it right every day. You need to occasionally go back to the Book and see what it says.

A gentle answer turns away wrath, but harsh words stir up anger (Proverbs 15:1).

In your anger do not sin. Do not let the sun go down while you are still angry (Ephesians 4:26).

He who answers before listening—that is his folly and his shame (Proverbs 18:13 NIV).

You're not to be like the man who said. "Last night my wife and I had words. Unfortunately, I didn't get to say any of mine!" That's not communication.

Listening to the other person matters and is probably the most important element in the communication playbook. Listening is not thinking of what you're going to say as a comeback while the other person is still talking. Listen! It's so important that you learn how to dwell with one another, how to get along with one another, and how to express love for one another.

Fourth: The Bible says that when you get married, your body is not your own anymore. Your body belongs to your mate.

The husband should fulfill his marital duty to his wife, and likewise the wife to her husband. The wife does not have authority over her own body but yields it to her husband. In the same way, the husband does not have authority over his own body but yields it to his wife. Do not deprive each other except perhaps by mutual consent and for a time, so that you may devote yourselves to prayer. Then come together again so that Satan will not tempt you because of your lack of self-control. I say this as a concession, not as a command (I Corinthians 7:3-6).

Two sweet ladies were talking, and one said, "I went out with Tommy last night. And I had to slap his face five times." The other lady asked, "Why? Did he get fresh with you?" The first responded, "No! I thought he was dead." Remember, your physical relationship is important. My Granddaddy Stone fathered 28 children. I can remember going to Granddaddy's house, and he'd come home from the sawmill dressed in blue overalls and a long sleeve collared black shirt, and he'd have on his black rim glasses.

His wife, Thelma (my grandmother), would be cooking. I remember one time sitting at the kitchen bar eating, watching my grandma cook. Granddaddy came in from work, walked over, right in front of me, and put his hand on her rear end and just started patting it. I hollered, "Granddaddy, I don't need to see this. I'm going to be scarred emotionally the rest of my life!"

That was his normal routine. He would come home from work and start patting her little bottom. He was 80 years old! But that playful, sexual, physical attraction kept their marriage together for years and years and years. It's important! We are all going to change physically. You may say, "I haven't changed." Now go look at the mirror and pull out some old pictures! It's called "the four B's" – baldness – bulges – bifocals – and bunions, and you have them all!

Here's the key to this whole chapter: Half the people I grew up with are now divorced, while Cherise and I celebrate our 29th anniversary later this year. We have history together. Sure, we've had rough patches. Some people glide into marital bliss, but we've had to work our way into there. We've had arguments that lasted too long, and we've gotten stuck in places that we should have moved forward in. But at the end of the day, we have decided "till death do we part."

I'm thankful that I have a family that is intact. It's not perfect, but it is intact. That means that my children can go to one set of parents. I don't say that meanly or harshly to those who've been divorced. If you've been divorced, God loves you. Stay open: He has a plan for you. But I'm thankful that we stayed together because our kids have seen a marriage in front of them that was not perfect at all, yet they have seen a man and a woman who made a commitment in Buford, Georgia almost 30 years ago. We said, "till death do we part." They have seen us keep it together through our struggles, and that is something that is extremely important.

You've made those same vows, and just like Cherise and me, your marriage is still a good idea. Your marriage is still the most important part of your life, and it is worth the time it takes to do it right. God has a plan, and it is my prayer that the two of you begin by renewing your commitment to God and to first and foremost growing in your faith. There are no marriage plans designed to make it to the cave of couples that do not involve you growing in your faith and in your relationship with Jesus Christ. Start there. He will guide you in the rest and prove to be a strong tower in times of trouble and a faithful Father in all seasons of life.

Encounter

What are you doing to grow in your faith together as a couple? Do you pray together, read the Bible together, worship together? What is the Lord saying to you about this in the marriage?

....

....

....

....

....

Engage

What are some things you would like to see change in your faith together as a couple? After you have answered this question pray about sharing your answer with your spouse. If you feel led and your spouse is open to it, answer this engage question together in the space below.

....

....

....

....

....

I have committed adultery several times in the past, but not any more. Should I tell my spouse?

My first question is have you been tested for a sexually transmitted disease? If not, do not have sexual relations until you do. My second question is, how do you know, "not any more?" My third question is how long ago are we talking? My fourth question is, are any of your previous partners in any part of you or your spouse's life in any way now? If yes, then absolutely you need to have full disclosure and end any form of a relationship with that person, including all social media.

If you have had an encounter with God that changed you and since that time there is no infidelity, then I think that is a conversation you need to have as a "new creation." And ask for forgiveness.

CHAPTER 15

The Three "S" Words That Must Be Addressed in Every Marriage

> "
>
> "If I had a flower for every time I thought of you...
> I could walk through my garden forever."
> —Alfred Tennyson
>
> "

Cherise and I have been married for nearly 30 years, and there is no one on this planet that I would rather do life with. But our early years were tough years. We were both drawing our own lines in the sand and there were days where I had my doubts, and so did she. I'm just being honest. I will be forever grateful to my mother-in-law Pat for taking such a strong stand in those early days. There were days when Cherise was fed up with me and wanted to just go home only to find a mother who would have no part of that. Pat would insist that she hang in there and work to find middle ground...and we did.

As I look back at those days I can see clearly that it was nothing more than selfishness that created that conflict, and more often than not it was me. When you go from a world where everything you have is yours to a world where nearly everything is shared, if there is any selfishness in you it will rear its ugly head in those first few years of marriage. There was...and it did.

Selfishness

As I study marriages, and as I look back at my own marriage, I know there is one topic that must be discussed and dealt with if we're going to hold our marriages together. It is probably more important than any other topic. The demise of families and marriages can all come down to that one word: **selfishness.** If a marriage fails, 999 times out of 1000, selfishness got in there somewhere.

I love to read Genesis 1 as God unfolds His magnificent plan of creation. Listen to these words. "God created Adam, male and female." At first glance, this is a strange verse, "So God created man in His own image, in the image of God He created him; male and female He created them" (Genesis 1:27 NKJV).

That's in the Bible. So, when God first made Adam, he wasn't just a man, but God put woman in him as well. This is profound. The first time I really studied this passage, I didn't realize specifically what it was saying--that He created Adam, male and female. God made him in His own likeness because God is all sufficient.

This is the picture of marriage. Marriage is taking two and putting them together to make one. "Now the two shall become one" is conjoining the two even though they have two minds, two hearts, two bodies, two ways of seeing things, two ways of communicating, and two ways of understanding. God says, in effect, that marriage is bringing you back to how I originally created you from the beginning. The two shall become one again.

Marriage and sexuality is about being with **one person.** We must get that message back in the church because our culture has lied to an entire generation and said that they can just do whatever they want to do and it doesn't affect them. And yet, God made us for **one person. One perso**n is called to walk with you through life, forever, into eternity…**one person.**

I believe that before Cherise and I were married and became one on our honeymoon, God had put us together in Heaven and had made us one. When we got married, the two of us came back together, joining back up. But the problem is there are two of us now. She just didn't jump back in me and do everything I wanted her to do.

Not too long ago I came across a video about the oldest conjoined twins that are still alive. Conjoined twins are so rare that there are fewer than ten known sets alive today. For almost six decades, their life has been a study in the art of cooperation and compromise. Their story is a tribute to brotherly love between Ronnie and Donnie and also their younger brother, Jim. They're sometimes their own worst enemies, but most of the time they're their own best friends.

Ronnie is very happy-go-lucky whereas Donnie is as serious and hard core as they get. They're total opposites. They're one person in their physical body, but they're total opposites in personality traits. But while the brothers' personalities are opposite, their hobbies are identical. They collect toy cars and both are devoted Dallas Cowboy football fans. They also both love watching TV, but they don't like the same shows. Usually the biggest arguments are over the TV, even though they have two now. If one turns his up, the other will turn his up even louder.

The terminology used to describe Ronnie and Donnie would be *omphalo-ischiopagus*. In other words, they're joined from the base of their sternum, which involves their bellies and then down into their pelvis, which is one big ring. There is a band of tissue about two to three inches wide that goes across their midline that they can both feel.

There's only one male organ and one rectum. Each has his own stomach and his own heart. They live on their own, but they rely heavily on their younger brother Jim who is also their best friend.

The closeness that Ronnie and Donnie share is not always a positive. Just think what life would be like if you took somebody, even the person you care about the most, and were chained to him 24 hours a day, every day for years, never being able to get away. Their whole life is a compromise.

This is a symbolic picture of what real marriage is. If you don't want that kind of life where you have to consider that other person all the time, every day, in every way, then you are neglecting the very food your marriage needs to survive.

Submission

The word **submission** is another dirty S word. Submission means structure. Somebody has to lead. Somebody has to open the door if you're going to walk through the door. Who's going to do it? If you're both always trying to have your way, someone is always going to be disappointed or frustrated or worse…checked out. The Lord said to me one day, "Ask the people 'What are you killing by being so selfish? What are you destroying in your home and in your family because of your defiance?'"

When you grasp that marriage is the two becoming one, you will see a difference in the atmosphere of your home. *Husbands, love your wives as Christ loved the church. And wives, submit to the husband*. Let him open the door.

Let me just say this, ladies. If one of those conjoined twins does everything, the other one's going to get weaker and weaker and weaker and weaker and weaker. So sometimes you have to stop and say, "You lead. You take the car down to the garage and you talk to the man that's trying to cheat us by charging us too much. You do it. I'm not going to do everything." If you want him to lead, then sometimes you have to say, "You do it." He may not do it the way you would have done it, but a greater good has been accomplished.

In marriage, you have to learn the art of cooperation and the art of working together because you're connected together for life. And it's going to be a miserable life if you don't start submitting to each other. If you have a son, you have to raise him to look for a wife, not a mama. He has to become his own man. He has to become the leader of his own household some day.

How do you do this? For Cherise and me, it means figuring out who does which things better. I don't get all caught up in stereotypes and macho posturing. There are just some things she does better and some things we can flip a coin on and usually she says, "You do that." You just learn who does what better. Maybe one of you needs to get out of the way and let the other go through the door.

Can you imagine being conjoined with another like these two boys were? Quit wasting your bullets on your mate and start shooting at the devil instead. Become submitted, one to another. One has to lead. Like conjoined twins – together we win, together we live, together we succeed. But if we're always fighting one another, we die. This is what marriage is.

It's a negotiation. It's the two becoming one. Unity means the two of you tie. The Bible said, *"A house divided against itself will not stand."* I'm praying that God will join you together while reading this book and that you will become your own dream team.

The scripture says three things about Adam when he was single. Number one: Adam was fellowshipping with God. He was in Eden, and Eden is not just a garden, but Eden was where God met and fellowshipped with him every day. The first need of man is not woman. The first need of man is to be with God.

Number two: Adam was alone; God looked at Adam and said, "It is not good for you to be alone." He had a relationship with God. In the cool of the day, he and God would walk through the Garden of Eden, talk, and just be together. But in the evening and in those dark watches of the night, he was all alone. If you remember your single days, you remember nights like this.

Number three: Adam had a job. God put him in the garden, and He gave him a job. That was not part of the curse, which would come later. People say that work is a part of the curse, but it wasn't. He gave the job before the curse ever began.

God said, "Cultivate this place. Take what I've given you and make it fruitful. Maximize the potential. Bring out the best in what I've given you." Ask yourself, "Is my spouse bringing out the best in me? Am I bringing out the best in my spouse?" God doesn't give you the perfect woman. God doesn't give you the perfect man. God will give you the raw material and say, "Now cultivate it. Bring out the best in each other, not the worst."

People think because they are saved, it's going to work out. They are so wrong. Just because someone is saved and the spouse is saved does not mean everything will just work out. Listen to what Proverbs 24 says: *"By understanding a house is built, and by wisdom it is established."* Both can be saved, both can love God, but if both don't get the knowledge of God's word daily, weekly, and throughout their lives, then they are again refusing to eat the very food that sustains the life of marriage. Go back to the Book!

I heard about a guy who got so angry at his wife he stopped talking to her. He had to get up and catch an early morning seven o'clock flight and didn't want to oversleep, so he wrote a letter and put it in an envelope and set it on her nightstand. It said, "I have an important meeting in the morning. You must wake me up at 5 a.m." The next morning, he woke up at 9 a.m. He was about to just blow a gasket and let her have it. He then discovered that she had gotten up and left a letter on HIS nightstand. It said, "It's 5 a.m. Wake up."

The silent treatment does not work! Get over it. The Bible put it like this in Ephesians: *"Don't let the sun go down on your wrath."* Just get over it. Forgive one another. Life is too short to go around ticked off all the time. Let me help you. Some of you started reading this book, or maybe even this chapter, angry with your spouse. Maybe you even had an argument today. Sooner or later, somebody has to say, "I'm sorry. I love you."

Two words that need to be cut out of our dictionary are – *impossible and divorce*. We don't have to have those words in our vocabulary. No marriage is so messed up that God can't heal, and nothing is impossible with God.

Sex

I want to talk just a little bit about **another S word called sex.** I am not an expert; I'm just going to tell you what the scripture says. This will help you if you will let it.

In Song of Solomon the 6th chapter, Solomon explains it. He says in verse two, "My beloved has gone to his garden, to the beds of spices, to feed the flock of the gardens."

He then describes how beautiful she is in ways that we don't understand any more. "Behold, you're fair. You have dove's eyes behind your veil. Your hair is like a flock of goats." That doesn't sound like a compliment, but it was. "Your beautiful black hair is just like a flock of goats. Your teeth are like a flock of shorn sheep which have come up from the washing." That's a nice way of saying you brush your teeth. And then, he says, "And every one of your teeth bears twins." In other words, he's saying, "You have all your teeth. I'm just thrilled with you."

He's praising her. "Your lips are like a strand of scarlet, and your mouth is lovely. Your temples behind your veil are like a piece of pomegranate. Your neck is like the tower of David, built for an armory, with a thousand bucklers and shields of mighty men hanging on it. Your breasts are like two fawns, twins of a gazelle..." This scripture needs to be discussed because if we don't own the subject of sexuality, the world and our culture will and it will be perverted and deranged.

One specific scripture says, "The marriage bed is undefiled." Another translation said, "The marriage bed is wonderfully creative." It should be. There are several reasons that God came up with the idea of sex; one is procreation and another reason is for our enjoyment and for our satisfaction. God is not a God who has a problem with you enjoying a relationship with your wife or your husband. Christian couples need to get free in this area.

I think the church needs to get out of people's bedroom. The bottom line is, the marriage bed is undefiled. It's your marriage. Establish your own comfort zones, and as long as there's not something violating scripture (like pornography or another person in the mix somewhere), it is permissible. Establish your own comfort zones, and if someone doesn't want to do something, that's where selfishness can enter and cause hurt and offense to creep in.

Cherise is the only girl I've ever slept with. I'm the only guy she's ever slept with. She is the standard for my beauty. I don't have to have the *Sports Illustrated* bathing suit edition to get excited, and I don't have to have Victoria's Secret turn me on. I don't have any secrets or a secret life. My wife is my standard. I like her. I want to look at her. She's crazy and she's a little wild, but there's nothing wrong with that. I don't need a pornography website. I have a wife who understands I have an eye gate and she has what these eyes desire.

I waited for 25 years, and it was worth the wait! God made sex for me and you to enjoy. And when we start having happy homes and marriages, then our children will see it and say, "I don't have to go sleep with 14 people. I want to be like mom and dad."

Some of you may feel shame trying to creep up on you because you have done something you know is sinful. Maybe you have looked at some things you know you had no business looking at...but remember that forgiveness, grace, mercy, and even restoration is yours for the asking. Grace makes all things new, the Bible said.

Men, we need to save ourselves as a locked up garden for our wives. We don't give ourselves to pornography, we don't give ourselves to websites, we don't give ourselves to craziness, and we don't give ourselves emotionally or physically to another woman (whether in person or online). We are to be a locked up garden. When we do those things, it will always be out of one motivation...selfishness.

Encounter

Although we talked about three S words, they're really all about one. Selfishness. Reflect below about what the Lord spoke to you in the previous chapter.

Engage

Have you truly put your spouse's interests above your own? Imagine if you both valued one another above yourself, would you not be equally satisfied? What is one thing you can do to let your husband or wife know you value their needs above your own?

When trust is compromised in a marriage, how do you go about learning to trust your spouse again?

More often than not, the first trust issue to be mended is your trust with the Lord. He sees all, and He knew and allowed it to happen. Make your peace there first. Have the conversations with the Lord and be completely honest. Every bit of confidence, security, and trust has to be rooted in your relationship with Jesus Christ. All other trust and love have to come from that place if it's going to come at all. Unconditional love is never easy, especially when given so freely, and then trampled under foot.

We are to forgive 70 times 7, which is so much easier to say than to actually do. But people do make mistakes. I recommend using a skilled marriage counselor to help you unearth the root causes for infidelity, if that was an issue. Not every indiscretion is the result of one person's selfishness. Usually there are other major factors that lead to the wrong choices in weak moments.

If you are the offending spouse you have to prove trust-worthy. You have to go the extra mile. Are you willing to stay off all social media? Are you willing to give your spouse your passwords for your cell and your computer? Are you willing to live a life "above reproach?" Are you willing to commit to investing your life into the life of the church? Are you willing to attend regularly? Growing in your faith?

Lastly, are you willing to connect with another person or group of same-sex people who can commit to holding you accountable? These are the kinds of things that re-build trust over time.

Section
05

Affair Proof Your Marriage

CHAPTER 16

An Ancient Story for a Modern Day Marriage

> "When you realize you want to spend the rest of your life with somebody, you want the rest of your life to start as soon as possible."
> —When Harry Met Sally

I want to ask you a question. Did you plan on getting married, popping out a few kids, and then getting a divorce? Let me ask it another way. Did you plan on, down the road at some point, having an affair? Did you know that nearly 100 percent of the people who start out in marriage never intended for those things to happen? And yet it happens. Why? I believe that the answer is because we live in a culture that does a horrible job preparing us for marriage. That's why I'm so excited to know that scores of singles are also reading this book. It seems like people are more prepared for divorced than they are for actually being married.

We live in a society that says "Date. If you really like them, hook up sexually to test your compatibility. And if you *really* like them and everything's going good, go ahead and move in together. Think of the money you will save!!! Just go ahead and put your toothbrush in the bathroom, move your clothes in the closet, and play house. You don't need a piece of paper to live like married people do. After all, it's just a ceremony. It's no big deal." At least, that's what the popular opinion is today in America.

Then the inevitable happens; trouble and conflict rears its ugly head, but hey, no problem! Just get your toothbrush and clothes and get out of there. Then start the process over in another relationship; move your toothbrush into another bathroom (that is, until you hit a bump in the road in that relationship). And then, here you go again. Try it here; try it there. By the time you finally get married, you have been so programmed to bail when tough times come that leaving is ingrained in the brain as normal.

Let's look at a couple in the Old Testament that had the worst marriage in all the Bible. But even at their worst, God said, "Don't get a divorce. I have something else in mind." The husband was a prophet named Hosea, and his wife's name was Gomer. Strike number one for the marriage was the wife's name: Gomer. All of us 40 and over are thinking the same thing: Gomer Pyle. A woman named Gomer? I don't care how you say it. You can use your sexiest Barry White voice and say, "I love you, Gomer." I don't care how beautiful or amazing she is. If her name is Gomer, there is going to be an issue at some point. Of course I'm joking, and I'm also praying that there is not a woman named Gomer who is reading this right now!

I like what the scripture said in Hosea. It said she was of the children of the "whoredoms." She was not just Hosea the prophet's wife, but she was also a prostitute. That was her heritage and the only life she had known.

There was this single man of God, the prophet Hosea, and he was just starting a church. Now this girl named Gomer who had a very bad reputation entered the picture. He was the new young pastor of this new church in the town and a bachelor, and all the women in the church wanted him to marry their daughter. But right in the middle of his search for a wife, God told Hosea to marry Gomer. Can you imagine Hosea's reservations and his confusion? "Her?! Gomer the prostitute?!" God's response? "Marry her." Hosea may not have trusted this command of God, but he did trust the God who gave him the command, and so Hosea grew to love Gomer as God put a love in his heart for her.

All Gomer knew was that, from Hosea, she received a kindness and love she had never known. She knew he was not like the other men who just wanted one thing. Hosea treated her with dignity. So when Hosea finally asked Gomer to marry him, she said yes. The perfect ending to a "rags to riches" story. The young prophet married the former prostitute.

As was the case in those days, it wasn't long until Gomer felt a little flutter in her belly, and she noticed that she was "with child." Nine quick months later, the baby arrived and life started. When life starts happening to a new, young preacher, it goes something like this: the church that he's been pastoring is really starting to grow. People are coming from everywhere. He's spending more and more time at the office. He's studying more. He's dealing with budgets, and boards, and people who are sometimes mean and upset. Eventually he has to hire some staff. So it was with Hosea.

Back on the homefront, Gomer was out of her element. This was all new to her. She wasn't raised to be a pastor's wife. She wasn't in the choir, and she never went to Sunday School. She just came from the street right into the ministry, and now, all these people were looking at her and talking about her because she wasn't fitting their image of what a pastor's wife should and shouldn't do. As the days went by, she saw less and less of Hosea as the weight of his ministry took priority over the marriage.

Like women through the ages, she began thinking that this was not fair at all. He was not helping her raise this kid, and he was always working while she was stuck at home raising a baby all by herself. She said what women have said for hundreds of years: "I didn't sign up for this; babies and diapers and screaming. Where is he? Why doesn't he take out the garbage? Why doesn't he show me any attention anymore?"

Hosea didn't know what to do because his father was absent from his life. Before long, they argued and were always on the other's last nerve. They always argued and fussed and fought. We've all been there, haven't we?

So, like any woman of her era, she goes to her Facebook – The Gomer Facebook Page! On her wall she sees something from one of her old boyfriends. He writes, "I've been looking for a girl named Gomer. Is it really you? Of course, there's only one Gomer on the whole internet." She accepts his "friend request" and the reunion is on. He asks, "Gomer! Is that really you?" She replies, "Oh, yes it's me." He asks, "Well, what's going on with you?" And she says, "Well, I married a preacher." He exclaims, "No, this isn't you! This can't be the same 'Gomer' I knew." She replies, "It's me alright. I married a preacher, and I've had a baby. How about you?" He continues the conversation, "I'm a personal trainer." They chit-chat, just like old times. Sound familiar? It should, because these kinds of online conversations are the birthplace for more infidelity and divorce than just about any other cause. Gomer gets a little more vulnerable and tells him that she really has let herself go and of course, he offers to train her for free, at his exclusive gym that has free childcare. Within months Gomer begins to have feelings for this Facebook flash from the past, and it's not long until she wants to take it a step further, and he is all-too-willing to comply.

What's Missing- The 80/20 Rule

Before you know it, Gomer has fallen for the greatest marriage misconception ever invented, and it can hit every one of us at some point in our marriages. The number one lie of Satan that she believed in the moment that she decides to stray was this: **What I am missing is better than what I have.**

Gomer had a decent guy. She had a good marriage. She had a good provider. Hosea had some great qualities and he loved her despite the baggage she brought to the relationship. He cared about her and he was a good dad. He brought home the check and he took care of her. He wasn't just a good man; he was a spiritual man. He loved God. He had some good things going for him, but she didn't focus on the good things. She said, "What I'm missing is more important in this moment than what I have." Her craving for the 20% that was missing made her blind to the 80% that was good.

In other words, what she decided to do is what so many decide to do. She made up her mind that she would trade in the 80% for the 20% that was missing. In most marriages, that spouse and that marriage is going to meet about 80% of your expectations. No person – no husband and no wife – will ever be able to meet 100% of your expectations.

The Bible doesn't tell us what 20% he wasn't giving her that the other guy seemed to have. Maybe it was that he showed her more attention, or maybe it was little love notes, or maybe it was that he complimented her. Maybe he had more money and was able to give her expensive gifts. I don't know what the 20% was for Gomer, but whatever it was, she was willing to gamble the 80% on the 20% momentary fix.

I've been pastoring for almost three decades, and I have lived long enough to know that you don't want me to counsel you. Thank God we have a counseling center at our church. I've had many a man look at me and say, "I'm leaving my wife." and I looked back at them, and said, "You're an idiot. A wife of 20 years, three children, a beautiful home, memories, Christmases, birthdays, family vacations, and the joy of a home? You're willing to risk all that?" Something happened to this deceived soul. He met a girl half his age, and she met the 20% of what was missing.

After I composed myself, I asked him why he would leave all that for this new fling. His response dumbfounded me. He replied, "I, uh – we watch – she likes the same kind of sports I like. We watch old movies together." And then there was the big one: "We have forbidden sex." This was a confusing response to me because marriage can't really compete with forbidden sex because there's no such thing in marriage as forbidden sex. The marriage bed is undefiled. That means it is to be wonderfully creative and fun. As long as the two consent, and there's nothing in the scripture against it, party on! But this man had found that one or two things his wife did not or would not do, despite the fact that she would do everything else!

I am always amazed at how many people trade the 80% for the 20%. What about you? Are you going to trade the house? The 20 years of marriage? The relationship with your children? Are you going to exchange the path they are on for a path that has historically led to some very bad places? Is it really worth all that? You're going to trade grandchildren and watching your kids get married for that 20%? If your answer is yes, then I have a word for you. If the grass looks greener on the other side, you need to start watering your own yard. If the grass looks greener on the other side, there might be a busted septic tank up under that other yard.

I'll never forget something I saw at my granddaddy's farm. I was leading a revival in his area and I had some free time, so I decided to go see him. After we walked for awhile, we came to the cow pasture. One of his cows had stuck his head through the barbed wire fence to eat the grass on the other side. The gap between the barbed wire fencing wasn't very wide, so each time the cow moved his head between the wires, the wire cut his throat. The more he moved – the more it cut his throat. As I stood there, I watched this cow cutting his throat more and more, all because he didn't want to eat any of the acres and acres of grass on his side of the fence. He only wanted the grass on the other side. More and more blood started trickling down and dripping off of the cow's chest. It was crazy! This cow had the same grass on his side of the fence; he just wanted the grass that he wasn't allowed to have!

I remember thinking, this is what people do with marriage. Instead of enjoying the entire field of grass on their own side of the fence, they would risk cutting their own throat to eat the little bit of grass they could reach on the other side. This is what Gomer did. She got bored and ran out, and she hooked up not only with this guy, but she hooked up with multiple men after him. She went back to being the old Gomer.

The book of Hosea is one of the greatest and most amazing love stories in the Bible. God, through the book of Hosea, tells the reader that this is what Israel has spiritually done to Him. They've been committing spiritual immoralities and spiritual adultery against Him. In the third chapter, God is voicing His anger with Gomer and His chosen people Israel. He's like a jealous lover, and He's angry.

If you have ever been betrayed or deeply disappointed with someone you love, Hosea is the book for you to read. It teaches that there are three stages that God goes through when we have pushed Him too far. **Stage one: He got angry.** He said, "You don't realize how I have taken care of you. You made a vow to me and you promised me you wouldn't serve any other gods. Yet here you are doing just that." He said, "I've taken good care of you, and you've broken my heart. You've devastated me. How could you do this to me?"

Then there's a sudden shift. In **Stage two: His anger elevated to righteous anger.**

Suddenly, He's so mad that He says it's over, and I quit. But then that love starts stirring, and it moves into righteous anger. You might have felt righteous anger before. Righteous anger is when you turn the anger off of the person, and you turn it toward the spiritual force that wants to devastate and destroy your marriage, your children, and your children's children. Then God begins to turn. There's something that happens when righteous anger shows up that says: Devil, if you think you're going to get this home, if you think this situation is going to destroy us, if you think this marriage is over, I have news for you. I'm going to fight for my marriage. I'm going to fight for my husband or my wife. I'm going to fight. This is the stage that I'm praying will envelope you. If you've been through a betrayal, at some point you have to put your focus on the real issue-- Satan--and move into righteous anger.

Stage three: He extended His unfailing love. God can get angry, but ultimately His unfailing love for you, the love of a father for His child, kicks in. This is when you begin to understand that you can't blame everything on the devil. The bottom line is that sometimes, people can do some very bad things and only unfailing, unconditional love can find a way to redemption. In Hosea 3, it is unfailing love that overwhelms the heart of God. In Hosea 2:19 Hosea doesn't throw a pity party or try to get even. Instead, he refuses to give up on Gomer. He says, "I will allure her and lead her into the desert –and speak comfortably to her." He then makes this profound statement. He said, "I will give her back her vineyards and I will cause, in the valley of Achor [which means trouble], there to be a door of hope." Does that sound like revenge to you?

This scripture is about a valley. The thing that you have to do when your marriage is in a valley of marital trouble is realize that God will always have a door of hope if you won't give up, if you won't quit, and if you won't walk out. He says He will put a door of hope in the valley of trouble for you.

Two Keys to Great Marriage

If you want to have a great marriage, there are two ways to do it. **Number one,** just do everything right. Be perfect. Don't ever say anything you shouldn't. Don't ever stay out too long and come home late. Don't ever do anything that upsets one another. In my life I've met a few people like that (or at least they project that). They're sweet, they're touchy-feely, and everything is just perfect all the time. I've heard people say, "We have never had a fight in 75 years." I want to say, "That's because you are wallpaper, buddy. You're a doormat at the front door of life."

But there's another way to have a great marriage, and this is the route my wife and

I have taken. **Number two,** it is to go through the valley of trouble **together.** You are going to get mad and be angry at one another, but eventually you will come under conviction. By Sunday, you have to make it right or there won't be an anointing.

I remember all of the stress and worry we went through as young parents. We all go through that. But here's what we've learned. When we go through the valley of trouble, we don't grab our toothbrushes and say it's over. We reach over, grab each other's hand, and we just keep pursuing God. Even in the lowest valley seasons of marriage, He will always bring a door of hope. I don't care how bad it gets. I don't care how dark it gets. I don't care how many demons you're fighting. I don't care how much sin has come into a home. There is a door of hope in every valley of marital trouble.

A Door of Hope in a Valley of Trouble

We all sin. We all mess up. We all make cruel comments. We all do stupid things. These things happen in marriage. In Hosea 3:1, God speaks to Hosea again, saying, "Start all over. Love your wife again, even though she's been in bed with her latest boyfriend. I know she is a cheater. Love her anyway. Love her the way I love you. Love him the way I love you. Forgive the way I forgive you. That's what I've done for Israel. That's what I've done for my people. That's what I have done for you." The amazing thing about this story is that there are no guarantees. We are never told if Gomer ever straightened up. It was a chance that he had to take, but taking a chance on a word from the throne of God is never a bad bet. Never!

Sometimes people do everything right and the marriage still goes through what it goes through because people have the power to make choices. I was thinking about how this chapter ends, because the Bible said that she was now used, abused, and afflicted; she was eaten up with disease and infected. The Bible even implies that she had a pimp. God told Hosea, "Love her again. Forgive her again. Your marriage is in the valley of trouble, but don't pick up your toothbrush and leave. I put a door of hope in the valley of pornography, the valley of financial difficulty, the valley of deceit, the valley of Achor." For some of you, the enemy has told you it's over. But God told me to tell you that there's a door of hope in whatever valley you are in or ever will be in.

The story ends in a very powerful way. Her pimp is selling her on an auction block like an animal, and God told Hosea to take his silver and purchase her back. He said to buy her with precious resources and take her back, love her, and walk through that door of hope that He put in his valley of trouble. Hosea obeyed the Lord and he bought back his wife. It's a beautiful picture of what Jesus Christ has done for you and me. When we are immoral, when we are filthy in sin, when we're infected with the lust of the flesh, the lust of the eyes, the pride of life, and anger – when we're infected with the filthiness of sin and selfishness, Jesus Christ paid the price. Jesus Christ went to the bank of Calvary and made a withdrawal from the riches of the cross and paid the price so that we could be cleansed and so that we could be forgiven and that we could be healed. He died so that we could be helped, that we could be changed, and that we could be whole again.

Encounter

There's a door of hope in any valley of despair or guilt or trouble. What is the Lord speaking to you about or bringing to your mind as a result of this chapter? Reflect on what you feel God is saying about your own marriage through this story.

Engage

What do you feel the Lord calling you to DO as a result of what you have read and considered?

The Bible says that the wife sanctifies her husband. What does this mean?

The passage is I Corinthians 7:14

For the unbelieving husband has been sanctified through his wife, and the unbelieving wife has been sanctified through her believing husband. Otherwise your children would be unclean, but as it is, they are holy.

Occasionally "sanctified" takes on a special sense. This does not mean that the marriage itself saves the non-Christian. If that were the case, the apostle would not refer to the union as that of a "believer" and an "unbeliever." Moreover, this idea would contradict numerous passages that reveal salvation must be accessed by **personal** *obedience (Acts 2:40; 2 Thessalonians 1:7-9; Hebrews 5:8-9).*

The sense seems to be that the unbeliever, being in close proximity with the Christian spouse, is in a sort of "set apart" environment — cut off from the total and extreme godless influence of the world. The end result is the happy possibility that the sinner may be won to the Lord through Christian influence.

W. E. Vine observed that "the unbelieving husband or wife is relatively set apart through his or her believing partner, and abiding in the natural union instead of breaking it by leaving, receives a **spiritual influence** *holding the possibility of actual conversion."*

CHAPTER 17

Affair Proof Your Marriage

"

"A great marriage is not when the 'perfect couple' comes together. It is when an imperfect couple learns to enjoy their differences." —Dave Meurer

"

There was a bishop who went to one of his churches on Mother's Day to observe one of his parish pastors. The young pastor was all set to preach his Mother's Day sermon as the bishop settled in on the front row. The preacher opened his message by saying these words, "I spent the best years of my life in the arms of another man's wife." He then paused and said, "My father's wife."

Everybody said, "Wow, that's really good. That's really clever. What a great opening." And the bishop thought, "That was a great opening. As a matter of fact, I'm preaching at another church tonight. I think I'll take that opening line and use it in my sermon tonight."

The bishop travels to another city and gets up in front of a whole new congregation, and he said, "It's Mother's Day, so I'm going to preach to the mothers. I spent the best years of my life in the arms of another man's wife." And then he paused…and had a total mental block, and it went on and on. He finally said, "And for the life of me, I cannot remember what her name was." That's not a good time to go blank!

The seventh commandment in Exodus 30:14 is "Thou shalt not commit adultery." Some people think that verse says, "Thou shalt not admit adultery." But that is NOT what it says--the word is COMMIT--not ADMIT.

Once there was a man who was convinced his wife was having an affair, and so he left work early to catch her. Sure enough, when he got to his apartment, he smelled the aroma of a cigar. Rage overcame him and he kicked in the door. He frantically went through the apartment, looking for the man who would have been in the apartment with his wife. He searched and searched but couldn't find a soul. He looked out the window and saw a man quickly getting into a sports car. Overcome by rage with his adrenaline pumping, he picked up the refrigerator and threw it out on top of the little sports car convertible. As he threw it out, though, the cord got wrapped around his neck and pulled him out the window with it. He fell four stories to his death. End of scene one.

Scene two finds him at the pearly gates of Heaven. Saint Peter asks the man, "Why should I let you in?" By now the man is an emotional wreck and he says, "I loved my wife. I was just trying to preserve my marriage. I was so enraged when I saw that other man in the sports car...I can't believe that I did what I did." Saint Peter said, "It's all right. It's all right. We understand these kinds of things. Just calm down." He turns to the second man and he says, "Why are you here, and why should I let you in?" He said, "I don't know what happened. I was just minding my own business. I stopped to get a newspaper, and when I got back in my sports car, the next thing I remember is a pain on top of my head."

Then Saint Peter turned to the third man and he said, "And you. Just what were you doing in that refrigerator?"

God knows everything, and whether you admit it or not, the Bible says, "Do not commit adultery." Adultery can vary from a casual fling online in a chatroom, to a full-fledged, ongoing affair. I read recently that 91% of the sexual encounters that you see on TV are people who are not married. The sex that is on television, implied or explicit, comes with a message that is constantly telling us that romantic love always leads to sex, and whether you are married or not is inconsequential. It is made to seem so innocent and so normal, and yet it's destroying families.

"Thou shalt not commit adultery." If one name stands out from the Old Testament as the most famous adulterer who ever lived, it would be King David. He lusted after Bathsheba, he acted on this lust, and the lust resulted in a pregnancy which led to a murder. As is so often the case, David's adultery drove him to lie and to scheme and to plot. And this little indiscretion, as the world calls it, became a full-fledged massive scandal that could have changed the course of David's life and even history itself.

Read the next few lines very carefully. After pastoring for almost 30 years, I have never met anyone who has committed adultery who did not regret it. Never. I have never met one man or woman who committed adultery who did not live to regret it, and regret it deeply. Adultery, even when forgiven, leaves a scar. Even in the 21st century, the wages of sin is still death.

The book of Proverbs is the book of wisdom. Chapters four through seven talk a great deal about the sin of adultery. It says, *"Can a man scoop fire into his lap and not be burned? So it is with the man who sleeps with another man's wife."* Listen. Playing with adultery is like playing with fire. It's like taking the bricks out in your basement of the bottom floor knowing that if you take one too many, the rest of the house might collapse. Playing with adultery is pulling that one brick that will cause the entire house to collapse.

"Whosoever" – it goes on to say – *"commits adultery is an utter fool, for they destroy their soul."* Adultery hurts. It shatters trust. It severs friendships. It degrades people. Adultery destroys families, defiles marriages, and defies God. Marriage is about giving; adultery is about taking. God, who designed marriage, said, "Do not commit adultery because it's a sin against marriage."

Sex is very powerful, and unless it's kept in the confines of marriage, it can explode into a destructive power that can destroy families and homes. Jesus said, *"You have heard it said 'Thou shalt not commit adultery.'"* Listen to this. *"But I tell you that anyone who looks upon a woman to lust after her in his heart has already committed adultery with her in his heart. So if your eye offends you, pluck it out. If your hand offends you, cut it off."* Do you take a second look?

A couple was in a shopping mall, looking at an item together, and a gorgeous woman in great shape walked by and the man immediately looked at the woman and followed her with his eyes until his head had nearly spun all the way around. As the woman walked out of view, the man turned back around and composed himself just in time to hear his wife say, "Was it worth it, based on the trouble you're in now?"

Adultery begins on the stage of imagination. **Before the enemy gets you in the bed, he has to get in your head.** And it all begins with a thought. That's what Jesus was talking about when he discussed the problem of a person lusting through his eyes. Jesus said if a person can't control his wandering eye, then he should "Pluck it out." The problem is, I still have another one and, knowing me, I'd look with the other one, too. He said, "If you sin with your hand, then cut it off," but I have another one of those, too!

Jesus is not saying a person should literally pluck his eye out or cut his hand off. He's saying that the problem is not the eye; the problem is the heart. When He says, "Pluck out your eye" he means to cancel your Playboy subscription; cancel your Swimsuit Edition; cancel some of the things you have been watching on your TV and on some of the satellite channels. Stop looking at some of the internet material you have been looking at. Get rid of it. Pluck it out of your life because adultery always begins with thoughts that can lead to actions that destroy your life. These assaults on our eye-gates are the enemy creeping into our homes using the eye gate and through technology.

Watch your words because they become thoughts. Watch your thoughts because they become actions. Watch your actions because they become habits. Watch your habits because they become character. Watch your character because it controls your destiny. Don't rationalize it.

In Psalms 51, after David committed adultery, he prayed this incredible prayer. "Cleanse me, O God, and take not Your Holy Spirit from me. Restore unto me, the joy of my salvation. And renew a RIGHT Spirit within me." Anybody that has messed up or that has in any way committed adultery should read Psalms 51 and ask God for cleansing. God answered it for him; He'll answer it for you.

A Happy Marriage

There was a little girl who went to Sunday School, and afterwards her mother asked her, "Well, what did you learn in church today?" The child said, "The Sunday School teacher told us about how God took mud and made man. Then God saw that man was alone and didn't have anybody to talk to, so he was very sad. Then God reached into man and took his brains out and He made a woman."

She didn't quite get the story right, but that would explain a lot, wouldn't it? Agatha Christie wrote, "An archaeologist is the best husband a woman can have. The older she gets, the more he's interested in her." (Yes, Agatha Christie was married to an archaeologist.)

My wife and I have been married almost 30 years. We met in church, and we've raised our family in church. We've not always had a perfect marriage, and there have been times when our marriage was very challenged and very, very stressed, just like everyone else's.

Some people act like marriage is just Heaven on earth all of the time. It's just not true. In real marriage, you disagree. In real marriage, you get on each other's nerves. In real marriage, the enemy will tell you, you were better off by yourself. But I'm telling

---

you, you can bury a marriage with a lot of little digs. There's no such thing as a perfect marriage because every marriage is the union of two imperfect people. Husbands, never criticize your wife's judgment. Always remember she chose to marry you.

A happy marriage is not how much the husband and wife are alike and think alike. A happy marriage is not how much you think alike or see eye to eye. If you don't see eye to eye, walk hand in hand until your vision becomes clearer and you can see that middle-ground.

A relationship guide called "A Man's Guide to Understanding Female English" explains just how differently men and women think. When a woman says "We need," what she's really saying is "I want." When a woman says "It's your decision," what she's actually saying is that the correct decision should be obvious to you by now. When a woman says "Do what you want to do," what she really means is "You'll pay for it later." When a woman says "I'll be ready in a minute," what she really means is "Take your shoes off and sit down and watch a TV show; you're going nowhere." When a woman says "You need to learn how to communicate," what she's really saying is "Just agree with me, you idiot."

All that makes sense to me, but there is also a second part to this relationship guide called, "A woman's guide to male English." When a man says "I'm hungry," he means "I'm hungry." When a man says "I'm sleepy," he means "I'm sleepy." When a man says "I'm tired," he means "I'm tired." But when a man says "I love you!" he really means "Can we have sex now?"

The guide goes on to say that the four hardest statements to make in marriage are: 1) I was wrong; 2) I am sorry; 3) Forgive me; 4) I need help. Use these statements often. Use them over and over and over. When you mess up, say, "I'm sorry. I was wrong." One of my favorite lines that I use is "I don't know what I was thinking." That'll get you out of almost anything. "I don't know what I was thinking." Men, that was just a little freebie to help you.

How to Affair Proof Your Marriage

Here's how you affair proof your marriage. **First,** always show respect; be more interested in fixing the problem than you are in avoiding the blame. Do you want to be reconciled or do you want to be right? Too many times, we spend too much time trying to avoid the blame instead of fixing the problem. Just fix the problem and quit fighting.

Second, take responsibility. The Bible said, *"Each of you look not to your own interests, but the interests of each other."* Major problems in marriages come from one foul word – selfishness. When you take responsibility, the entire atmosphere changes.

Third, romance. If there was more formality and even old fashioned "courting" in marriages, there would be less marriages in court.

Remember how kind and tender you were to each other when you were dating. You anticipated the date with excitement. The Bible said, "May you rejoice with the wife of your youth...may you ever be captivated by her love." You couldn't wait for the call and you couldn't wait for the date and you couldn't wait for the time together. "May you rejoice in the wife of your youth...may you ever be captivated by her love." When you dated, it was fun. If we don't watch it, the fun goes out of our marriage.

We need to cultivate romance again.

Respect, responsibility, romance, and **fourth,** resolve.

A brilliant 60-year-old university president was thriving in his career. The university had grown and become strong and healthy under his leadership. His wife developed Alzheimer's, and after much thought and prayer, he handed in his resignation to the board. The board of directors could not believe someone of his great potential – really just hitting his greatest days – would resign to go take care of a woman who had developed such a bad case of Alzheimer's that she didn't even hardly know who he was most of the time.

At the board meeting where they discussed the president's resignation, one of the board members spoke up and said, "Why are you doing this? It's noble and we understand that you love your wife, but you must realize, she doesn't even know who you are." After thinking for a moment, the president said, "That may well be true. But I know who she is, and I made a commitment to her, a promise, and a vow that said 'in sickness and in health, till death do we part.' I don't have to spend this time with her; I CHOOSE to spend this time with her."

The trying times are not the times to stop trying. They're the times to grab hold of one another and remember the words you said before God... "For better, for worse; for richer, for poorer; in sickness and in health; to love and to cherish." I want to give you those words again because you said them before God. You made those vows before God – "To have and to hold; for better, for worse; for richer, for poorer; in sickness and in health; to love and to cherish, 'till death do we part."

Marriage will have to endure storms. That will require great resolve. You will have to face things together, and the enemy will do everything he can to destroy your marriage, your family, your purity and your children. It's not just a battle about you and your wife; he's out to destroy your children and your children's children.

Leonardo Da Vinci said, "An arch consists of two weaknesses which, leaning one against the other, make a strength." That's what marriage is. The starting point of a powerful marriage is when you acknowledge, "God, I need You. God, without You, I am selfish. I will not do what I should do and be what I should be."

I made up my mind many years ago that my family would never have to walk around this town and hear people snicker because their daddy couldn't keep his zipper up or because he couldn't live a life that would bring honor and glory to Jesus Christ. Adultery starts in your heart. It starts through the eyes and through the ears and through the lack of connection with one another. The greater the threat is out there, the more we need to come together in our homes, in our marriages, and in our families.

We need to say to the spirit of the age, that seducing spirit, "You will not have our marriages. The longer we live, the stronger we'll get because we're better together." It takes a made up mind to live a holy life in the generation that we're living in. You must be deliberate. You must make up your mind, "The seventh commandment will be lived every day of my life." Thou shalt not commit adultery.

Encounter

Jesus said, "You're building your life and your family, either on sand or you're building it on the Rock." None of us have a perfect family or perfect marriage, but what we do have is a perfect Savior. He takes our imperfect lives and holds our families together. He's brought you here, to this book, to awaken in you a new purity; to awaken in you a new commitment and consecration to your marriage.

....

....

....

....

....

Engage

Which of the four R's do you need to focus on most in your marriage right now? Respect, responsibility, romance or resolve? What actions will you take to make it a priority?

....

....

....

....

....

....

I am in a ministry that deals with crisis. This can, on occasion, extend beyond the regular hours and even into weekends. How do you balance ministry and marriage while needs are critical and spill into your couple time and feeling like a failure?

This one is easy: Get over yourself. You are not their savior and you are not what they need. It can feel, in ministries like this, that if you don't drop everything and run to the rescue, there will be a disaster. But in doing that, if this is truly a ministry, you forget that God knows, God hears, and He has a plan.

He also has a plan for you. His plan includes wisdom and knowledge and margin for your vocational calling, but His greatest priority is not your vocation. It's your marriage and your family. When you get these out of balance for an extended period of time you will find yourself neck deep in vocation, but coming home to an empty house. The ministry field is littered with the neglected spouses and children of great pastors and missionaries. I have determined my children will NOT be a part of that carnage. And so should you.

CHAPTER 18

How to Outlast Your Toughest Season

> 66

"Love does not consist of gazing at each other, but in looking outward together in the same direction." —Antoine de Saint-Exupéry

> 99

Psalm 1:1 is one of the most powerful passages of scripture in the Old Testament:

Blessed is the man that walks not in the counsel of the ungodly, nor stands in the way of sinners, nor sits in the seat of the scornful. But his delight is in the law of the Lord; and in his law doth he meditate day and night. He shall be like a tree planted by the rivers of water, that brings forth fruit in his season; his leaf also will not wither, and whatever he does will prosper.

If you are going to make it in this world and in your marriage, you have to learn some secrets for "outlasting your toughest times." What do you do when your 401K has fallen like an egg from a tall chicken? What do you do when you've been laid off, and you don't have any income? What do you do when your family is under siege? What do you do when the world seems like it's ready to explode?

I love to study David because he wasn't always happy. The David we see in scripture was not a one dimensional person. He had a full range of emotions and dealt with more than his share of highs and lows. He wasn't always happy, nor was he always sad. One moment he was on top of the world and the next moment he felt like it was caving in on him. This wide range of emotions happened many times in his life. That's why I love the word of God and why it is still as relatable today as it was back then.

You can hit a season where everything is going so well that it can make all the little problems you have seem like nothing. Then there are the tough seasons that redefine what "tough" is. When you're in a "tough season" your perspective about everything changes. I once saw a pastor get down on the floor--laid completely out to illustrate the point that when you are down that low, everything looks different--out of order even-- and larger than it does when you are standing up straight. Some seasons make you think that you'd give anything to have those old little problems back when they are weighed against those of the heavy and dark season.

When you're in a "tough season" none of the clichés, platitudes, or one-liners will work on you or your problem. Have you ever had people try to cheer you up, and when you tell them all that you're going through, they say stuff like, "Well, just let go and let God." Have you ever just wanted to let go on their head?!?

Why Do the Wicked Prosper?

To make things even more difficult, it seems that when you are at your lowest, wicked people prosper like never before. That can be so discouraging if you don't stop and consider God's word. God knew we would struggle with the temptation called "comparison." The Bible is quick to remind us that *"with the wicked it is not so, for soon, they shall be cut down like the grass!"* Don't be envious of the wicked when they prosper. Don't be envious of the wicked when they multiply because God sees what's happening, and God avenges, and God will take up your cause. Just keep your eyes on the Word of God, and you'll make it through the tough seasons! You have to be like a tree. Sometimes the tree is fruitful, and sometimes the tree looks withered. But if you're connected to the River, you'll make it through the dry season and will come back again! You'll bring forth fruit again! It is not so with the wicked, for they will be cut down like the grass.

Have you ever noticed that a "tough season" seems to last a long time? You can handle the tough stuff for a while, but sometimes it won't go away, and just when it seems like it's over, it comes back again. That's when it's so good to know God's justice and His mercy is such that *"He sets an end to the darkness."* You're just in a tough season, but the good news is that it's going to end. It's a season and not a sentence.

Welcome to the big league! You've graduated out of Christianity 101, which means that you are going to encounter tough seasons in this life. It's the tough seasons that causes so many to fall away. That's when people start going back to their old iniquities and sin, forgetting the one hundred reasons they left that past in the first place. That's when you find out if you're in a "covenant" or if you're just in it for the fun and the blessings.

Self-Doubt

One indicator that you are in the midst of a tough season is that you begin to lose your spiritual confidence. It's been said that tough seasons do not define us...they reveal us, and they have their place in shaping and molding us into His plan for our lives. You know you're in a tough season when it brings you into a mentality of **self-doubt**. This is big.

Tough seasons always push and push until they move you into self-doubt. Some things will hit you and make you doubt who you are...doubt what you believe...doubt your own ability, and worse yet, doubt His ability to pull you through it. It seems like it's double jeopardy when you are already in a low season, and then even bigger hits come. I've had some things hit me when I was already in the "tough season," and if you aren't careful, you find yourself in a season of self-doubt. Did I make a bad decision? Should we have waited on that campus? Should we have made that major purchase? Was that the right hire? Was that the right decision? Should I have said that?

Even when I know I heard from God, and I know that I have made the right decision, a week or a month or two later, I will go through a tough season and then all those questions start attacking me. I'll hear little voices in my head that say, "You're a failure. You're stupid. What a joke! You call yourself a Christian? What kind of preacher are you? That was a horrible decision. What were you thinking!" Self-doubt! That's why Psalms, chapter 1 is so powerful, because it says,

"Blessed is the man who walks not in the counsel of the ungodly, nor standeth in the way of sinners, nor sitteth in the seat of the scornful. But his delight is in the law of the Lord" – listen, now here it is – "and in it doth he meditate day and night."

The word **"meditate"** is very interesting. In the Hebrew language, it literally means "to self talk." In other words, to talk to yourself. It's not enough to read the Bible in the morning and in the night. You really begin to get victory over "self-doubt" when you have an ongoing monologue in your head, constantly rehearsing the truths of God. You learn that in the "tough seasons" of life, you have to "meditate" and "self talk" because your words have the power of life and death whether talking to someone else...or to yourself.

Start Talking

You have to literally start talking to yourself. You don't have to do it outwardly, but you must do it on the inside. You're either going to have overcoming talk, or undergoing talk! You're either going to have victory talk, or defeat talk. You're either going to have blessing talk, or cursing talk in the monologue in your head; the dialogue that's going on in your brain. You say to yourself, "This is not going to last forever. God's Word is true. Yes, I'm a man of God. Yes, I love the Lord. I may not have everything going right, but I know I'm saved. I won't doubt my salvation! I won't doubt that God is with me and for me!"

You know you're in a "tough season" **when Heaven is silent.** As humans we have come to know that one product of human nature is that if somebody's mad at us, they quit speaking to us. And so, in our human minds, we assume if God is not saying anything or we aren't feeling His presence, He must be mad at me. He's getting me back. He's punishing me. He's angry with me.

It's critical that you understand God's Word on this. That is NOT how God operates. You're just going through a "tough season." You need to understand a very critical spiritual truth. **When the teacher is silent, it is because he's giving a test. And the teacher never talks during a test.** The teacher will teach you all week long, and then say, "The test over everything is Friday." So if He's giving you a test, it just proves that He has already given you every thing you need to pass the test.

But the question is, "Are you going to be a sponge that just hears a bunch of sermons or are you going to pass the test by getting a hold of what God has told you and put your knowledge to the test?" Can you stand in the valley and say, "That valley belongs to praise! I'm chasing after Goliath with my praise!" Praise Him, especially if you're in a "tough season" – especially if Heaven has been quiet – especially if you've been doubting yourself.

Don't Give Up

Don't lose your way. Don't fall aside. Don't give up. God has not left you unprepared for your "tough season!" David was anointed by Samuel, and immediately his brothers rejected him. Immediately he began to face battles. A lion tried to kill him, a bear tried to kill him, and then Goliath came. Then Saul got jealous and tried to kill him. Then Saul's army chased him for years. All of these issues seemed so daunting and so unfair to David. If only David knew what I want to teach you right now, oh the heartache he would have not had to endure. If you can ever grasp a very simple spiritual truth, it will change the way you look at everything. David wasn't going through a series of injustices and unfortunate events. Simply put, God was preparing David to be a king.

The same thing applies to your life. You have not gone through what you have gone through because of a series of unfortunate events...ever. God has been preparing you for your assignment. I've learned some lessons about these seasons of tough times. **I've learned that the blessed man talks to himself. That the blessed man meditates and says what the Word says about him back to himself.**

I've learned something else. I've learned that the blessed man "does not walk in the counsel of the ungodly." If people are telling you to do anything that would disobey the Word of God, don't listen and don't hang around. The blessed man is the one who walks not in the counsel of the ungodly! And anything that is not in this Book is ungodly! Don't go there.

Planted Like a Tree

Scripture says, "The blessed man is like a tree." Now if you're going to be blessed, you have to get a revelation of a tree. Why a tree? Trees go through more than one season. If you just take a drive around your city any time in the spring or summer you will see beautiful and amazing trees. But those leaves on those same trees are going to fall. Those same trees, when fall comes, are going to look like they have withered up and died. Outwardly they will look like they are dying because cold weather comes to trees. We are like those trees. Cold weather and stormy seasons come, and there are parts of the year when everything seems to dry up and die.

Why does cold weather come? It doesn't come to kill the trees but if the cold didn't come, then most trees would die because the insects and other things that feast on those trees would kill the trees. They're dependent on trees for their survival! The insects that would eat it to the core, die during the winter. The cold only comes to preserve the tree!

Later Not Now

We all have freezers in our homes. You put things in the freezer you want to eat at a later time. It's not that they're not valuable and it's not that you don't want them. It's not that they're not important, but you just don't need what they offer you now, so you put them in the freezer so that they will be preserved for another day.

The same is true in our walk with God. If you're going through a deep freeze, and it feels like you're forsaken by God, it's not that God doesn't love you, He's just saying, "Later, not now. You're going to have another season, and I'm getting you ready for it. You're going to hit levels you've never hit before, and do things you've never done before. You are going to know joy like you've never known joy before! You are going to dream dreams you've never dreamed before! But it's later, not now!"

Planted in Marriage

The blessing of the Lord is to be planted in one marriage, one man with one woman, through good and bad, through cold seasons, through fruitful seasons; planted in a church, planted in a ministry, planted in the word, planted in faith! You have to be like a tree that's planted by the river, drawing from that river. You just keep drawing, even when you're not producing, you keep drawing from the river!

Keep talking to yourself. Get up and go to church. Anytime the devil gives you his top ten list why you shouldn't go to church, that's a sure sign there's something waiting for you at that house that you need. Talk to yourself and say, "Get your tail out of that bed; you're going to God's house!"

If you are in the freezer it's because you are about to hit a new season. If it's cold it's because that new season is coming and you are about to be more fruitful than you've ever been. Your best days are yet to come. Don't you walk out of that situation. Don't you give up! Be like a tree and stay planted!

I want to share this powerful statement with you, *"Do not forsake the power of partnership."* This is something the Lord spoke to my heart and I feel like it something we all need to be reminded of:

"One can chase a thousand . . . When you're in a tough season, you don't need to go through it alone. Just get two or three people you can really trust. 'If any two …' That's the power of partnership. If any two or three of you will agree, it shall be done! One shall chase a thousand, two ten thousand. Don't forsake the power of partnership."

Your church is that place of partnership, if you will make it a priority. If "tough times" are coming against your family, and your finances, it's all Satan's attempt to divide and break up the power of a partnership between a husband and a wife, and between you and your church. So reaffirm your power of partnership with your husband or your wife. I don't care what you're going through, you have to say, "Baby, we're going through it together!" Get to your church as a family, and create some new habits and some new traditions.

You have too much fruit coming down the line if you'll just hold on. He prepares you for these times and He's prepared you for these times. Your God is faithful.

I have written a prayer that I would like you to read for your life. I want to encourage you to allow it to saturate your being:

I speak peace to your mind. Sometimes your mind races all the time. I speak peace to your mind. May the Holy Spirit soothe and minister to your troubled mind. Sometimes you have seasons of silence and it seems like the Lord is so far away. I speak to your ears to be opened to hear the simple word of encouragement. May you survive your "toughest season" in Jesus' name. I speak to someone who feels surrounded and outnumbered. I say "the Lord rebuke you Satan, in that home, in that family, in that financial crisis."

Every spirit that's bringing trauma, nightmares, and fear, I bind you in Jesus' name. I rebuke every demonic power that's robbing you of peace, and rest, and faith. I command self doubt to be defeated, with self talk that comes from God's Word in your life. That mentality that causes you to doubt your own ability, we crush it in the name of Jesus. I speak peace. You will survive these "tough times," says the Lord. You're like a tree planted, drawing from the river. And you will produce fruit again abundantly. Whatever your hand touches will prosper again, saith the Lord. Another wave of prospering the work of your hand is coming, if you can outlast this "tough season."

Encounter

Take a moment to reflect below on what the Lord may have been saying to you in the previous chapter.

_____

_____

_____

_____

_____

_____

Engage

What are some things you can do right now related to what your have read and encountered in this chapter?

_____

_____

_____

_____

_____

_____

Real Solutions

One of today's well-known Christian leaders encourages us to ask, "What is the wise thing to do?" Is there a single question you would suggest couples ask as a filter for overcoming conflicts, disagreements, and arguments?

Yes. Is this worth the fight? And here are a few tips I'll offer for working through conflicts as well:

1. *Think it through.*

2. *Seek to understand more than to be understood.*

3. *Let them finish.*

4. *Don't always respond with the first thing that comes to mind.*

5. *And here is the big one: there are always two sides to every story. Sometimes three—yours, mine and the truth.*

6. *Pray, and then watch to see what God does next.*

Section
06

Bonded Together Forever

CHAPTER 19

Remove the Gates—Remove the Barriers

> **"**
>
> "A happy marriage is the union of two good forgivers." —Robert Quillen
>
> **"**

Marriage is a choice. Nobody made you walk down the aisle. You went through the gate of marriage, and you said, "I vow before God and witnesses to stay together for better or for worse, for richer or for poorer, for fatter or for skinnier, for meaner or for sweeter. In sickness and in health, as long as we both shall live." You told the entire world, "I enter into this relationship with this person who will be the only one who will satisfy me, who I will sleep with, and who I live with for the rest of my life. I promise to You, God."

Years later, if yours is like 99% of every marriage that ever was, you look at that gate of marriage you walked through and you notice the hinges swing both ways. The same gate that got you in opens to let you out. The first thing you need to do is remove that gate and put up a wall where the gate was located. You need to say, "I got in, and now I'm sealing this sucker up because I'm in this for life."

Hollywood lied. Cinderella lied! All those fairy tales don't quite give the full picture. There's no such thing as "happily ever after," at least not the way we see it in the movies. I love my wife and she loves me. But by now, she has learned that the "'me" she married is really different than the me she has grown to know. By now, she knows I'm not a prince, and that while I can be charming, most of the time I'm just a regular guy. You learn and you grow and you allow for the imperfections in your partner because there are just as many imperfections in you.

When you first start out, you don't want to go anywhere or do anything. You just want to sit in each other's lap and stare into each other's eyes. You just HAVE to be together. After a while though, life sets in and you have to find compatibility in a wide range

---

of areas. Then you have a little argument, and you learn that there are some areas of interest and some things your spouse does that really start to get on your nerves. That's where you have to have the wall up instead of the gate.

Don't let the world lie to you about what love is, because if you leave your marriage thinking you will find a new and improved lover, guess what's going to happen? The National Survey of Families did a survey of 5,232 American adults about the state of their marriage. 1,315 of these people, approximately **one-fourth, described themselves as "unhappy and/or unhappily married."**

Five years later, the same organization tracked down all of those unhappy people to see what had happened to them and their marriages. Not surprisingly, many were divorced, although a considerable number had worked through their problems, and were still with the first husband or wife. Now here's the big surprise. Only 19% of those who were divorced now described themselves as happy. In other words, over 80% of those who divorced STILL considered themselves to be unhappy. They bought into the lie that said, "If I can just get out of this marriage and find me somebody that loves me, I'll be happy." For over 80%, that simply didn't transpire.

What about those who had decided to stick with it? Nearly eighty percent of those now said they were happily married and were much happier than they had been five years before when they were having severe problems.

Did you know that 60% of second marriages end up in divorce court and 75% of third marriages end up in divorce court? How tragic for those who have bought into the lie that the grass is greener elsewhere. You need to declare today, "As for me and my house, we will serve the Lord and this marriage is 'till death do we part.'"

As a father, I feel like I have fallen short in many ways, and I don't know any father who doesn't feel the same way. I know I'm flawed, but so are you. One particular time when I was feeling this way, I took a pen and a note pad and I asked myself, "What would make me a success as a father?" There are people who write books about perfect marriages and perfect fathers, and I think to myself, "Who are these people?" I don't know about you, but I have no interest in reading those books. They paint a picture of a husband and a dad that I could never be. I don't know how to get there, and even if I did, I don't think I could. I don't know anyone who thinks they can either.

Being a husband and a father can get messy. I have days when I'm mean and when I'm ugly and when I'm not nice. I have days when things get on my nerves a lot easier than other days. When I'm under pressure, I sometimes take it out on those I love the most. I hate it, but I just do. And truth be told, so do you. I don't like it, but that's how I am sometimes. Then I'll go crawl off in my office somewhere and die again, because I have to preach.

I recently had one of those weak moments when I could feel that negativity creeping in, but in that weak moment I felt like I heard the Lord speak to me, and He said, "Here's what I have called you to do as a father. You have two responsibilities: Number one, make sure that your family has a relationship with God, through Jesus Christ. And number two, pour into your kids self-esteem through affirmation." This simple direction and word from the Lord has made a huge difference in my approach and my focus when it comes to my children. It will for you as well if you will see this as a word for your family as well.

I love my church and the people I have come to know and love. But if I had to choose between these people and my church, or my family, there would not be a moment's hesitation. My children, my wife, my family…they come first and I would choose them every time, and so should you choose yours.

I remember asking, "God, what is success?" The Lord said, "You will be a success if your children have a relationship with Me. And if you poured self-esteem into your children by affirming them, blessing them, speaking words of encouragement, and loving them, consider yourself a success."

James Dobson said, "For every negative that you speak to your spouse and your children, you're supposed to pour five positives into their life." That really got to me, because I'm good at finding the negative. But for every time we're negative, even if it's justifiable, we're supposed to pour in at least five positives? Yes – "Do you know you're incredible? Do you know you're beautiful? Do you know how much you mean to me? Do you know that you're smarter than I'll ever be?" That's what I'm talking about. Words like that. "Do you know that I think you're incredible? I believe that God has such a plan for your life. There's no telling what you're going to do. You're going to do great things. You are amazing."

I want to go to my grave some day and be able to say, "I've done what I was supposed to do as a husband and as a dad." I don't know about you, but the older I get, the more this stuff weighs on my heart, and maybe it's because I am learning that I won't have them as close as they are right now, and neither will you. There will come a day when I won't hear those feet walking upstairs or those moments of laughter. The time is coming when our living room won't be filled with the whole family hanging out watching TV, just talking. The day will come when I will miss sitting in a room while everyone is on their cell phone. A day is coming when these halls will be silent and the sound of my children's voices will not be heard throughout the house. No hair dryers running, no doors opening and closing, no hustle and bustle of the morning. That day will come way too soon.

One night my son, Drake and I ate at Chili's. As we were leaving the restaurant, a young teenage girl backed up, pulled out, and drove just ahead of us. As Drake and I looked over we noticed there was an oncoming car going about forty-five miles an hour. I could see what was about to happen and started screaming, "Jesus, Jesus, Jesus, Jesus," and then BAM! They hit head on, and it was a terrible wreck. Drake and I ran over and helped the girl out of the car. The people in the other car were lying on the side of the road, bleeding. Thank God, after all was said and done, everyone was OK. As far as I know there were no major injuries, even though both cars were totaled. But it dawned on me in that moment that Drake and I could be laughing and talking one minute, and then just that quick, eternity can come!

Encounter

Does your family know God? Do you have a relationship with Him that they can follow after? Are your actions and your words leading your spouse and your family closer to God? Reflect below on these questions and anything else the Lord showed you through this chapter.

Engage

Take a moment to reflect on how your day-to-day choices impact the atmosphere of your home. Is there anything you feel the Lord nudging you to change or do differently?

My husband and I are going on 8 years divorced. I'd love to get back together but he is hesitant. We have 4 grown children and I never stopped loving him. We are even coming to this conference. I have invited him for the last 8 years and he finally said yes. Should we give marriage a second chance?

No, you should not give the past a second chance. You ended the past when you signed the divorce papers. If you hold out any hope at all to be married to the same man, it must be on completely new terms. Who are you both today?

I realize that you share children, and that is a factor. But you both have to answer a few very basic questions before you make this leap, or you will end up right where you ended the last time. 1. What were the three main reasons for the first split? What is different now in those three areas? 2. Name three ways that you are different today than you were when you split. 3. What is the opinion of each of your children? Of the two or three people that know you best, what do they think?

Any hope for a new relationship must not be based on old feelings because we always remember things better than they actually were. What is different now? What does your pastor think? Take the time to answer each of these questions before taking a step down that aisle again, and allow the Lord to show you what is true today.

CHAPTER 20

Bonded Together Forever

"

"Grow old with me! The best is yet to be."
—Robert Browning

"

Imagine for a moment that behind me there is a unity candle, and then imagine lighting it. You have probably seen these unity candles at weddings...maybe even your own. Most weddings that I have performed have had a unity candle, and I have seen a few variations on how these are used. I've seen the couple light it and then blow out their individual candles to represent that they are no longer two separate individuals, but just one. It really is an amazing thing when the two flames become one in goals and dreams and in spirit and emotions. It's a powerful, powerful thing.

Love always starts out in the infatuation stage. When you first see that person, you think it's love at first sight. But it's really not love at first sight, it's infatuation at first sight. All you can see are the similarities. But at some point, the relationship moves from that infatuation stage to the next stage of the relationship. At some point you have go deeper than that first phase of the relationship called "infatuation."

When you first get married, the passion of love and the light burning in the home for one another is so awesome. It's the "honeymoon stage" of marriage, and it is amazing. But if you stay together awhile, there comes a time when the giddy feelings begin to subside as the reality of actually living together sets in, and the thought of living with someone who squeezes their toothpaste from the middle as opposed to from the bottom up becomes no longer "cute!"

Maintaining the fire in marriage takes work, attention, and care, or else the flame could go out. When the fire goes out, cold begins to set in. There's a powerful scripture in Revelation 2:4-5 that I want to focus on. It says, *"...nevertheless I have this against you that you have left your first love."* Then it says, *"therefore remember from where you have fallen, repent and do the first works again or else I will come quickly and remove the lampstand from your place unless you repent."*

Notice that it says, "I'll remove the *lampstand."* He was talking about the church, and the lampstand that he was referring to was the Menorah that was in the Old Testament tabernacle. Pay attention to this. Jesus said, if you don't do three things – if you don't **remember the height** that you have fallen and how much your love used to burn for me, then insensitivity has begun to set in. If your passion level for me has fallen then your attention will be on other things as you grow colder and colder. If you grow cold, simply **repent** of it quickly and start **repeating** what you did when we first met, when you were so infatuated with me, or I will come and take the lampstand out of that church.

The lampstand represents God's hand of favor and blessing upon the church. God said that if you don't **remember** the height that you came from, **repent**, and then **repeat** – start doing your first works over, do what you did when you first fell in love with Me – then I'll take the light out.

The Three Roles of the Unity Candle Lampstand

The unity candle is the lampstand in a marriage. The lampstand provides three things. First, **it provides light**. When the light goes out in a marriage, you can't see yourself together long term. When the light goes out in a marriage, you can't see a future for your marriage. When the light goes out in a marriage, you can't see where you're going, and you can't even see yourself happily married years from now.

The second thing that light does is it **provides warmth.** This speaks of the emotional connection that we're supposed to have in marriage; not just the sexual heat, but the emotional warmth. Guys right now are tuning me out because they say, "I don't care much about the warmth, the emotional stuff." But here's the deal. If you don't have light and you don't have warmth, then you don't get any fire. Fire is the sexual passion, and if you lose the light and you lose the emotional connection in a relationship, it's a matter of time before the fire goes out and you're not touching one another and you're not intimate with one another. Remember the height from which you have fallen.

The third thing the light does is that it **adds value** to the marriage partner. In other words, you have to value the person God has given you. When you value your spouse, you bring the lampstand back to your marriage. When you stop valuing one another, God said, I will take the lampstand out of my church. The same is true for a relationship. When you stop valuing one another, treasuring one another, respecting one another, honoring one another, its value is decreased.. Dr. John Goodman said that he could predict divorce almost 100 percent of the time after meeting with couples for only 30 minutes, and his accuracy rate has been proven. He said "All I have to do is see whether or not they honor, respect, and value one another." If you're going to have the lamp burning in your relationship, you have to light the candle of value.

I heard a story about a Polynesian island and how it used to be when someone wanted to marry one of the young girls. The tradition of culture said that a suitor had to go to the father of that young girl and show him that he loved the daughter by giving the dad a gift. Then if he chose to, he would release his daughter. The only thing that was valuable on the island was cows. So if you were a beautiful girl and the young man wanted to marry you, he would take two to three cows and give them to your father, and your father would give you to be the bride.

There was a girl on the island--an ordinary, nice girl, but she wasn't a cover girl. A guy went to the dad and said, "I want to marry your daughter, and I brought you ten cows." Ten cows! Nobody on the island had ever paid ten cows for a girl. It was unheard of. Everybody thought he was crazy. She's just an ordinary girl, and he paid ten cows. But he knew exactly what he was doing because three months later, when she was walking around town, she walked around with her head held high. He made her feel so important that everywhere she went, everybody on the island would turn and say, that's the ten-cow woman. He gave value to her. He knew exactly what he was doing. Do you treasure your spouse? Do you truly value your significant other? Do you know there are eight chapters in the Song of Solomon, and Solomon praised her 40 times in these eight chapters?

Unchecked Fire

The sexual passion of a marriage is beautiful. Fire can warm you and cook food for you. Fire can be used for wonderful things. It can either warm you or it can burn you. And fire of sexual passion is meant to be kept inside of the marriage. If you've ever been camping – you know you have to build a barrier around the campfire so that the fire doesn't get out of that circle. One spark of fire that goes outside that circle can set the whole forest on fire.

We have a church in Orange County, California and a couple of years ago I would travel to speak nearly every Sunday night. I will never forget flying in there one Sunday afternoon to preach. The entire area of Southern California we flew over was black. All we could see was smoke, and houses by the hundreds were being burned. What a tragic scene that was.

All it takes to destroy a marriage, if you don't protect the fire of sexual passion in a marriage, is one little flame, one little flicker, that jumps out of the circle. One little flirting text message, one little flirting Facebook post can be tragic. This stuff matters. Guard the fire. Protect the fire of your relationship because it can burn down homes. One spark can burn down homes.

What if we've done our best and we've failed? There is the power of the Holy Spirit. There is Jesus at the center of our marriage, and at the center of our family, and at the center of our home. I'm not saying that you'll be perfect. I'm not saying you're not going to have storms or that you're never going to have an argument. But if you keep Him in the center, and you keep these promises and these fires lit that I just taught you about, the unity candle will stay in your home. The unity candle will stay in your family.

Marriage is like a dance. Have you ever seen these ballroom dancers? Anytime people dance that close, especially when they are just learning to dance, they are going to step on each other's toes. It's just a matter of time. That's what marriage is like. Unfortunately, that describes many marriages today. At one time, they were dancing. At one time, they were happy. But when the enemy comes, he takes the dance, he takes the music, he takes the joy out of the relationship. And it happens because we keep stepping on each other's toes, and we offend one another. We get mad at one another. You have to learn how to deal with conflict real quick. You have to handle it. You have to learn to deal with stepping on each other's toes.

Here's what the Holy Spirit wants me to tell you: **every marriage goes through the delight stage, every marriage goes through the disillusionment stage. But if you'll hold on,** if you'll keep loving one another, if you'll lead in forgiveness and humility and honesty, if you will light these candles that I am talking about, **you'll move from the delight phase to the disillusionment phase to the destiny phase of a marriage.**

If I had married any other girl in the world I would have missed the destiny God had for Cherise and me. She had to be the one. God put her with me, and me with her. I believe marriage is more than just two people falling in love. When God is truly in the center of a marriage, there is a destiny that is attached. My children have a destiny. My family has destiny. This church was waiting on Cherise and me, and that was our destiny. God honors a commitment and any time you make a commitment and a vow, you have to honor that vow. It matters. Even if the circumstances were not right but you came together anyway, you still say, "Lord, we honor you in this marriage." When you do this, Jesus comes right in the center and says, "I honor commitment."

The destiny of your marriage is at stake. The destiny of your children's future is at stake. The destiny of God's purpose for your life is at stake. You can't just walk away. You can't just give up, and if you'll hold on, and if you'll work on it, God will meet you there and make a way, even when there seems to be no way. You have taken a mighty step because God wants to move you from that disillusionment to absolute destiny in your marriage. Do you believe it? There is a prophetic destiny on your marriage.

Pray this prayer:

Lord, I give you my marriage. I thank you that you know how to move us into that purpose, that destiny, and I give you my marriage. And maybe the lampstand is just barely flickering or maybe even blown out. Maybe there's been some stuff that's happened and the lampstand is gone. But, Father, don't remove it; bring it back. Bring the lampstand back. I know it all starts with that center candle: you, Jesus. If we can get you, then we can fulfill this covenant and these promises. I give you our marriage. I give you our home. Help us to value one another. Help us to provide security and faith in all the things, Lord, that we need. Let us continue to burn in unity in our marriage.

Encounter

Take a moment and reflect on this chapter. What is the Lord saying to you about your marriage?

_____

_____

_____

_____

_____

_____

Engage

Which of the three: honor, respect, or value, do you feel is lacking the most in your marriage? How will you help add more of this to your relationship?

_____

_____

_____

_____

_____

_____

What are some practical steps you take to ensure that your marriage continues to grow and not plateau?

First of all, we take time out from our busy lives and do things together without the kids or any other distraction.

Also, I always have to remember I am thinking for two. Everyone has values, but there are some values that are your highest and most important values, and these can be different for every person. I think a high value for me has always been privacy and independence. I spend time with the Lord in the woods or on the lake or in my study every week, and I have for many years. In my alone time, I can find myself weighing out situations or decisions and then start to take steps only to find out I have violated one of Cherise's high values, which is respect and to be included and viewed as an equal partner in the decision-making process. We all have high values that we view the world through and when we don't honor those, we can offend and shut down relationship without ever intending to do so.

Finally, I believe that there is a great parallel between your married life and your spiritual life. If your marriage life is plateauing then there is a very good chance that your spiritual life has plateaued or even declined as well. The two go hand in hand. If you are both growing in your faith and drawing near to the Lord, then you are naturally drawing nearer to each other. It's geography.

CHAPTER 21

Balancing the Family Circus at the Speed of Life

"

"In all the world, there is no heart for me like yours.
In all the world, there is no love for you like mine."
—Maya Angelou

"

The Ringling Brothers have coined the phrase, "The Greatest Show on Earth!" I believe that marriage is the greatest show on earth. It is the best way to do life. Finding the mate with all of the challenges that come with living together and raising a family and staying together year after year after year is the greatest way to do life, and marriage is absolutely the greatest show on earth. I believe that with all my heart.

I'll speak for our own life and say that, at times, my family absolutely resembles a circus. With five children and my wife of nearly 30 years, the definition "a traveling company of performers, may include clowns" would fit us just fine. We fit every descriptor -- "performers, trained animals, tightrope walkers" -- that's our family, and probably yours as well. They say the most important person under the big tent in a circus is the ringmaster. He's the one that can bring order out of all of the sordid mess that is going on under the big tent. It's the ringmaster that has the greatest impact on the show.

When you go inside the big tent to see a circus, you see the trapeze artists as they are swinging back and forth, effortlessly. I thought about how that speaks of marriage. You'll see one swing out, with no net, and make the catch time and time again. That's what Genesis said marriage is. *"For this cause, a man will leave, or 'let go' of his father and his mother and cleave unto his mate."* Like the trapeze artists, it's complete and total trusting. The real foundation of marriage is trust that there is absolute commitment. Marriage is commitment on steroids. Marriage is saying absolutely, "I can trust you, and you can trust me."

You might have married him and imagined swinging out, and when you first caught him, he was a 32 in the waist, but now you swing out and he's a 42 in the waist. But trust and commitment says "I won't let you go. Even if the load's a little harder on my arms, I won't let you go. I love you." It's not just about the physical attraction in a godly marriage. It's about "We are committed and you can trust me."

Maybe when he grabbed you or you grabbed him, he had a lot of money. Perhaps he was a lot heavier because of the bank accounts and the tremendous job and the successful business. But maybe that all changed when the economy took a hit. Maybe it would be so easy now, because he's so much lighter, just to let him go. But this is what marriage is. It's when you can completely trust one another no matter what…and get to a place where it's not ever going to be about the stuff.

I was talking the other day with an NFL football player who attends our church, and he told me a startling thing about NFL football players. They make huge amounts of money when they're playing. But he said that 78% of the NFL marriages end when the check stops coming and the football player retires. How tragic and how defeating… and how empty is that kind of love. True love is like that trapeze artist at the circus. It's swinging and letting go and grabbing hold and sticking like glue and saying, "Whatever comes our way, we are in this totally, completely."

I thought about the guy who walks across the tightrope in the circus. That's how marriage feels to me sometimes. He has a balance beam and is trying to walk a tightrope. And he has to balance job demands and deadlines, and all of the kids' activities going on. Then, somehow, I'm supposed to have a prayer life and read the Bible and be involved in church. Somehow I'm supposed to take care of myself physically and I need to work out because I don't feel good anymore. Life is like I'm on a tightrope, constantly having to balance everything.

Marriage is like a circus and you're walking on a tightrope. And sometimes everything can get out of balance. You have to get the right balance. You have to learn how to balance your checkbook and your finances. "Are we going to make it to the end of the month? Are we going to make it through this crisis? Are we going to make it through this fight?" Because it's a tightrope of forgiveness. You're constantly having to balance your life and it's give and take, and sometimes you slip and you have to get back up. But you keep moving. It's a balancing act to keep our homes together, to keep our marriages together, and to stay balanced.

You know, some people are so spiritual. But those who are spiritually mature will tell you, that marriage is not spiritual all the time. Some of you know how to have heaven in church but hell at home. Things can get out of balance. I'm all for church. My God, I'm a pastor! I should be all for spirituality. But I've seen people get this thing all out of balance and there is a difference between spirituality and hyper-spirituality. You can't always have only the spiritual all the time. You have to be balanced. Marriage is balance. Marriage is having fun, too. Marriage is going on dates not just, work, work, work… church, church, church.

I was reading Acts chapter 10 recently. There's a man in that chapter named Cornelius, and the Bible said that he began to pray for his family day after day after day. And I want to say this: When I'm talking about balance, some of you are real good at praying, but not so good at showing affection.

Guys, I know that far too many men say, "I'm just not into prayer that much." But I'm telling you, you need a balance, and there's something about a man that prays for his family; prays for his wife and his children, and really prays and calls their names out. The scripture said in Acts 10:4 that *'Cornelius' prayers came up before God as a memorial for his whole family.'* Maybe you're in this situation now and you have children who are driving you crazy. You talk a lot about all of the stress in your marriage. Maybe you've hit a season when you're rearing children and everything's just kind of out of control. God said, *"Cornelius, your prayers have come up before me as a memorial."*

Every time you pray, God's stacking one prayer for your family on top of the other. Sometimes we think God's not hearing our prayers and they're not working and the kids are going crazy and the marriage is in the dumps. But you just keep praying. God hears your prayer! Every day of your life call your children's names out and call your spouse's name out; call your grandchildren's names out. Your prayers are never unanswered, they're just being stored up as a memorial, getting higher and higher and higher before the throne of God for your family. Your prayers are affecting generations.

One of my favorite attractions at a circus is the lion tamer. He'll come out with that lion, or those multiple lions, and have them sit on top of those platforms. Each lion must weigh more than 600 pounds. Those lions could take that lion tamer's head off. They could kill him if they wanted to. But he has a whip and he keeps them in place with that whip as he gently reminds them who is in control. Those lions are dangerous and could get loose. They could wreak havoc under that tent.

The Lord spoke to my heart, and He said, "Remind the people that there are lions in your home that want to devour your marriage and devour your children." That's a very serious warning to anyone reading this book. The key to keeping your marriage and your family intact is to keep the lion tamed.

You may be asking what I mean when I say, "There are lions in our home and we have to keep them tamed?" If there is a cell phone or any form of online technology in your home, then there is a lion in your home. As parents, Cherise and I want our children to have a cell phone so that if we are ever needed, they can contact us. We all need these. But with this simple object in our hands comes the internet and some pretty dangerous lions that want to get loose in our home. If you Google the name "Jesus," 416 million sites will come up but if you Google the word "porn," 951 million sites will come up, and on any iPhone device we are never more than a word or two away from any kind of pornography we choose…lions. We better make sure we keep the lions in our homes tamed.

How crazy is it that your spouse can get addicted to online porn right in your own home, right under your nose? Technology -- we want our children to have the internet for variety of good reasons. As adults, we need it for our professions and relationships, but we better never turn our back. Be accountable to one another with technology because it's devouring homes. It's corrupting and destroying homes and minds and marriages by the millions. Give the devil a cell phone and he will come into your home as a devouring, ravenous lion, and it's not long until secret sins begin to come into the home.

Team Up

Nobel Peace Prize winner Dr. Roger Sperry is recognized in the world of medicine for his scientific breakthrough studying how the brain functions in males and females. He found that in the 16 to 21 week period of gestation, boys have a chemical reaction in their brain that girls do not have. This stops the development of the right side of the brain. This isn't the same as the female brain. Dr. Sperry confirmed what every woman already knows: All men have brain damage. He received a Nobel Peace Prize for that discovery. The left side of the brain is logic; the right side of the brain is caring. What Dr. Sperry discovered is that men think more on their left side of the brain than the right side while women think more with the right side of their brain. Thus the difference in the way men and women see the world and interpret everything that happens.

Despite our differences, if you're going to have a successful marriage, you have to learn to "team up." Cherise and I have some friends that we've had for many years. We vacation a lot with these friends, and they have become our marriage mentors. You need two kinds of marriage mentors. First, you need an older couple, and second, you need a couple more your age. For our older couple, that has been T. F. and Thetus Tenney. One time I was just in my office and Brother Tenney called me on the phone. He said, "Jentezen, I don't commit adultery for two reasons." He said, "Number one, because God is against it. Number two, they tell." I've never forgotten that. We need people like this in our lives to speak truth in ways that make sense...timeless truth.

You also need some friends that are kind of at the same place in life that you are. They're raising teenagers just like you and you keep each other sane, because if they're a real friend, they don't act like their kids are angels and yours are demons. They will be vulnerable enough to say, "Well, honey, I know. We're going through the same stuff." There are few people with which you can share stuff like that and walk through life.

There's something about best friends. We all should have other friends, but when it comes down to it, there's nobody else I had rather be with than my wife. A three-fold cord is not easily broken. God is at the top, the husband on the left, the wife on the right, and notice that the closer that they get to God, the closer they come together. The reason some of you can't have intimacy and get close is because both of you are not climbing up that mountain to get to God. Just like the diagram at the beginning of Section Two, the more you draw near to God, automatically the closer you get to one another. This is the key. The further you get away from God individually, the further you begin to drift as a couple, no matter how successful you are in other parts of your life.

For Our Holiness

I want to close with this final truth about marriage. Marriage is not just for our happiness; it's also for our holiness. Cherise and I have had arguments that have lasted too long. We've been stuck in places before and just hunkered down, bitter and hurt at one another. We've had times, to be honest, through the 25-plus years and the raising children and building churches, that it seemed like the merciful thing -- I'm just being honest -- would have been to pull the plug a few times on our marriage because we were so opposed and opposite. And I said, "Lord, did I marry the right one?" And I'm sure she said, "God, I *know* I didn't marry the right one." All real marriages have those days when you just feel like, "God, can this work?"

I'm so thankful that I have a family that is an intact family. Notice that I didn't say a perfect family. I'm so glad that my children have one set of parents. I'm so glad that I have my wife by my side.

Dr. James Dobson, who has a national family ministry and daily radio program, read the following in one of his national broadcasts. It's a letter written by a 17-year-old girl to her father who was in the process of leaving her mother and family for another woman.

"Dear Daddy, when you walked away from mom and the family, you never knew the pain we felt. It's like we were all driving down the road one day in our car, mom in the front seat, me and Tommy in the backseat, our family was safe and secure. We knew whatever came around the curve of life, as long as you were behind the wheel, we were safe. Then that day it happened you left us. And, dad, I feel like I've been in a horrible wreck. I just want to wake up and it all be over like a bad dream. It's like mom has taken over the wheel and she's trying to drive and make the family work, but it's not the same. She's scared, she's afraid and alone and she cries at night in her room. I feel like, dad, we're going around a corner and all of a sudden -- we were going around the corner and all of a sudden our family had a head-on collision. And just before the crash I looked up and I saw the other car coming, speeding recklessly, dead-on for us. What was worse, I could not believe what I saw, you were behind the wheel of that other car, dad, and sitting next to you was your new girlfriend. While you were laughing and happy and she was all over you, you wrecked our world, dad. Mom's hurting so bad. We try to help, but all she does is lie on the side of the highway and bleed and cry and say, 'Why, God?' Tommy's pretending like he's not hurt, but he's withdrawn from all sports. He keeps himself isolated from his friends. He's getting angry, dad. I wish I could help him, but I'm wounded and I'm injured with my own hurts and I can't seem to get up. I have a question for you, dad. Did you get hurt at all in this wreck? Because it doesn't seem like it. Do you feel like we feel right now? If you do, I want to extend to you an invitation to come back home. Life will never be the same without you, dad."

This letter had one of the largest response of anything he had ever done on the program. I'm glad that I can report to you that when that letter was read by her father, it melted his heart. He packed his bags and went home, and when his wife opened the door, he fell to his knees and wept. Broken, he begged, "Please forgive me." That letter has been used to touch thousands and thousands of people. Maybe it was sent to touch you.

Maybe you are reading this while all hell is breaking loose in your home. Maybe the lion is devouring your children with drugs and alcohol, and the intimacy and passion for one another is gone. Maybe the friendship is gone. Maybe the years have eroded your love for each other. Maybe the lion has eaten everything.

In the story in the Book of Amos, the shepherd walked over and redeemed the ear and the leg. If that lion has gotten loose in your marriage, notice what he said; all you need to get it back is an ear and a leg. As long as you have an ear that can hear and a leg that will stand on the promise that God can restore what the lion has devoured under your tent, He can heal your marriage. He can help deliver your family and He can restore what the lion has devoured. And all it takes is an ear to hear it and a leg to stand on it and a husband and a wife who allow Jesus to be the center. Let's climb this mountain. The closer the wife gets to God --- and the closer the husband gets to God, automatically they begin to get closer to one another. He really is the center of it all. He really can restore what the lion has devoured.

Let me close by saying that the time you have taken to read this book has been a divine appointment. Even as you finish this book I believe a miracle in your marriage and in your home is happening. That's what happened to Cornelius. The Bible said the Holy Spirit fell on his whole house and restored everything. I'm going to go on and say what I feel: the Holy Spirit can come upon your whole household and affect everything in that tent. I am believing with you for the Holy Ghost to fall on your house and on your marriage. Make God be the center of your life. Just take a moment and focus on Him. I heard the Lord clearly say in my heart that this book would affect generations. If a mom gets saved, if a husband gets saved, if a marriage doesn't end in divorce … it will affect generations.

Encounter

Take a moment to reflect on this last chapter. What parts spoke to you the most?:

....

....

....

....

....

....

Engage

What are three things you feel God has spoken to you through this book that will help improve your marriage? Write them here and look back on them as a reminder when you need it!

....

....

....

....

....

....

Final Reflection

I challenge you, in these last few moments together in the Spirit, to say this prayer aloud.

Lord Jesus, I give You my life. I give You my marriage. I give You my family. I give You everything. Right now, Holy Spirit, take my life. Wash me in the blood. I receive Your forgiveness. I receive Your mercy. I receive Your grace. Bring laughter back to our marriage. Bring joy back to our relationship. Bring back the friendship between me and my spouse.

Jesus, I put You at the center of it all.

One Marriage…tried and true.

Resources

- The Definition of Modern Marriage by Maggie Reyes. http://modernmarried.com/how-to-re-define-marriage/#sthash.OImWLUL4.dpuf

- Yahoo Answers Forum https://answers.yahoo.com/question/index;_ylt=AwrXnCVTVjZXgX8A.mJPmolQ;_ylu=X3oDMTEydDZvcDhvBG NvbG8DZ3ExBHBvcwMxBHZ0aWQDQjA2NzJfMQRzZWMDc2M-?qid=20091228121515AAUhfQl

- Sara McClanahan in her article entitled The Consequences of Single Motherhood http://prospect.org/article/consequences-single-motherhood

- Fewer than half of U.S. kids today live in a 'traditional' family By Gretchen Livingston December 2014 http://www.pewresearch.org/fact-tank/2014/12/22/less-than-half-of-u-s-kids-today-live-in-a-traditional-family/

- The Sun, UK Edition, Rumpy Slumpy. Jasper Hamill. Dec 1, 2016, Porn Addiction Is Turning Men Into Hopeless Lovers Who Can't Satisfy Their Partners.